D0499847

Upper Covington Flat

JOSHUA TREE NATIONAL PARK

A Visitor's Guide

Robert B. Cates

LIVE
OAK
PRESS
Chatsworth, California

2nd Revised Edition....1995

Library of Congress Catalog Card Number 87-82023
ISBN 0-9619128-1-2

P.O. Box 3311, Chatsworth, CA 91313-3311

Printing by Delta Lithograph, Valencia, California.
Maps by Robert B. Cates.
Photos by the author unless noted otherwise.

TO MAUREEN

For her sustaining love and understanding
of my desert love affair

&

THE SIERRA CLUB

Which introduced me to my wife-to-be
and the wilderness beauty of the California desert

&

JUDY, JIM, AND ELDEN

For transforming a
National Monument
into a
National Park

ACKNOWLEDGMENTS

The following persons and institutions assisted the author in his research on Joshua Tree National Park. First and foremost were the staff of the National Park Service, administrators and guardians of Joshua Tree National Park, particularly former Superintendent Rick T. Anderson, former Chief Interpretive Officer Bob Woody , and Rangers Penny and Dennis Knuckles. The author wishes to thank all the staff of Joshua Tree National Park for their many courtesies over the years and for making available the extensive research library maintained at Park Headquarters in Twentynine Palms.

No one is more thoroughly versed in the history of the Twentynine Palms region and the story of William F. Keys and the Desert Queen Ranch than Art Kidwell, who so generously shared his hard-earned knowledge with me. Art is a writer-historian whose boundless energies extend beyond writing at a desk or searching through libraries. I cherish the hours we spent on the trail sharing the wonders of Joshua Tree as much as the facts and figures we sifted through while conducting formal research.

My introduction to Joshua Tree occurred on youthful camping trips with my parents, who nurtured my life-long respect and love of nature. I rediscovered the park through the Hundred Peaks Section of the Sierra Club, which has at least five 'on the list' park summits. My appreciation must be extended to the Sierra Club leaders who so kindly shared their knowledge and guided my footsteps on many expeditions to Joshua Tree National Park.

Once I began 'official' work on the present volume, several Sierra Club friends provided me with help and companionship in exploring on foot the many sites of interest within the park. Chief among these experienced outdoorsmen were Howard Howell and John Land; others who joined me at one time or another were Gordon Fisk, John W. Robinson, and Wes Shelberg.

Information about the Joshua Tree region is not commonly found on the shelves of the local library or bookstore. The author's literary awareness and library were expanded through the help of Glen Dawson, of Dawson's Book Shop in Los Angeles. A veritable mother-lode of historical information has been gathered and maintained by the Twentynine Palms Public Library.

CONTENTS

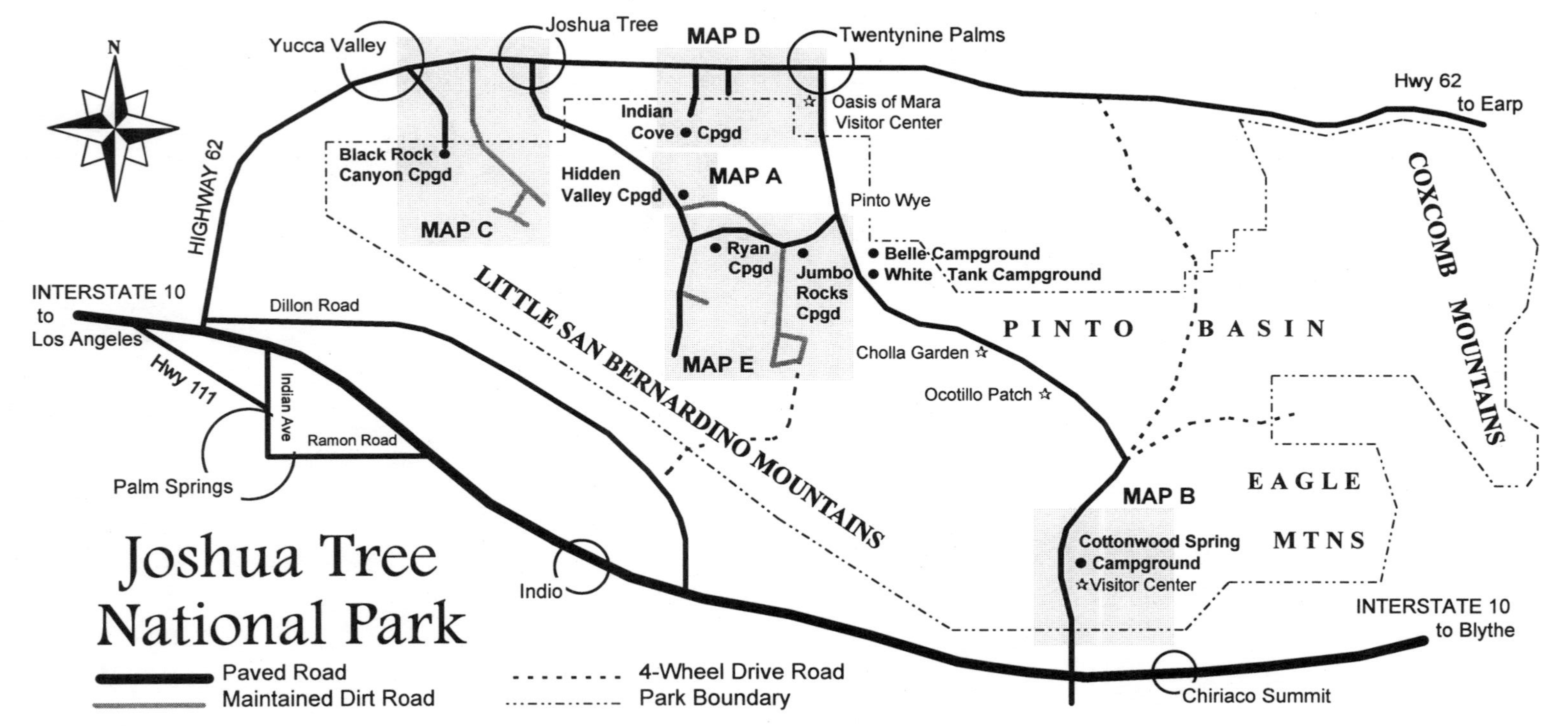

Joshua Tree
National Park
N
Yucca Valley
Joshua Tree
MAP D
Twentynine Palms
Hwy 62
to Earp
Oasis of Mara
Visitor Center
Indian
Cove Cpgd
Black Rock
Canyon Cpgd
HIGHWAY 62
Hidden
Valley Cpgd
MAP A
Pinto Wye
MAP C
Ryan
Cpgd
Jumbo
Rocks
Cpgd
Belle Campground
White Tank Campground
COXCOMB MOUNTAINS
INTERSTATE 10
to
Los Angeles
Dillon Road
PINTO BASIN
LITTLE SAN BERNARDINO MOUNTAINS
MAP E
Cholla Garden
Ocotillo Patch
Hwy 111
Indian Ave
Ramon Road
Palm Springs
MAP B
EAGLE
MTNS
Cottonwood Spring
Campground
Visitor Center
Indio
INTERSTATE 10
to Blythe
Chiriaco Summit
Paved Road
Maintained Dirt Road
4-Wheel Drive Road
Park Boundary

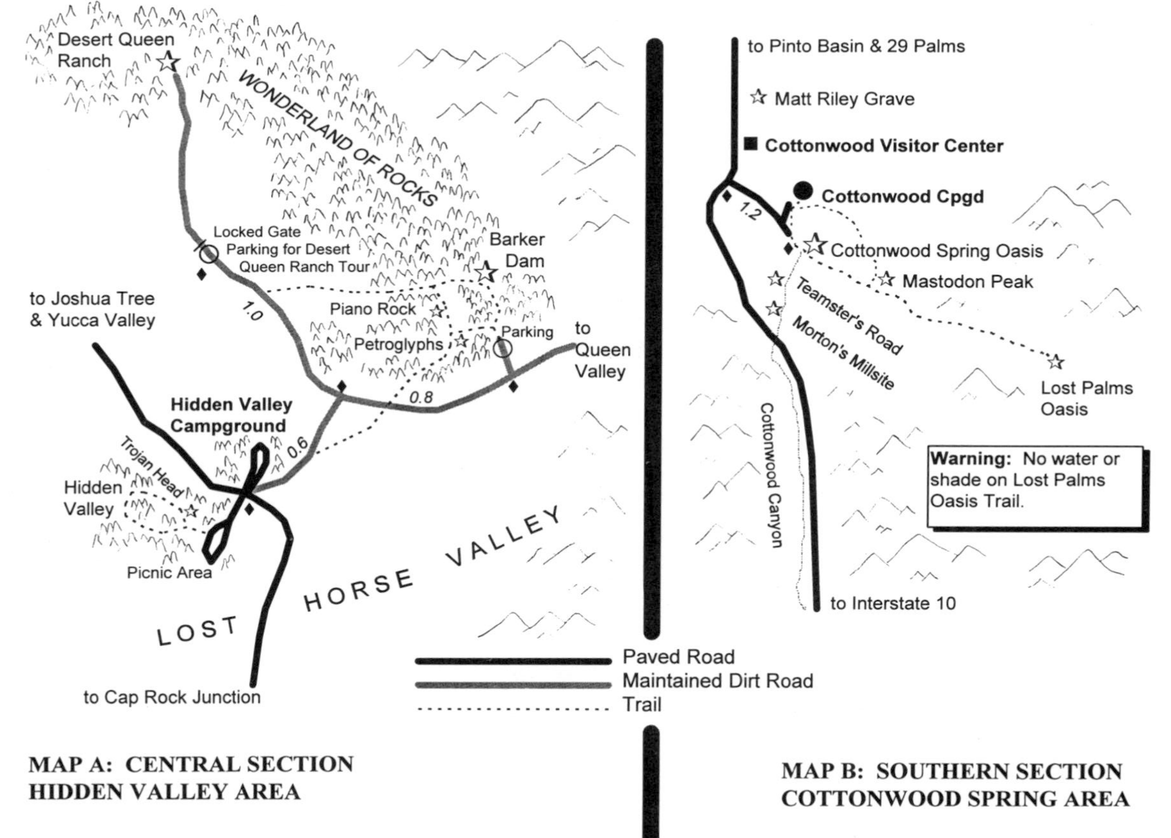

MAP A: CENTRAL SECTION
HIDDEN VALLEY AREA

MAP B: SOUTHERN SECTION
COTTONWOOD SPRING AREA

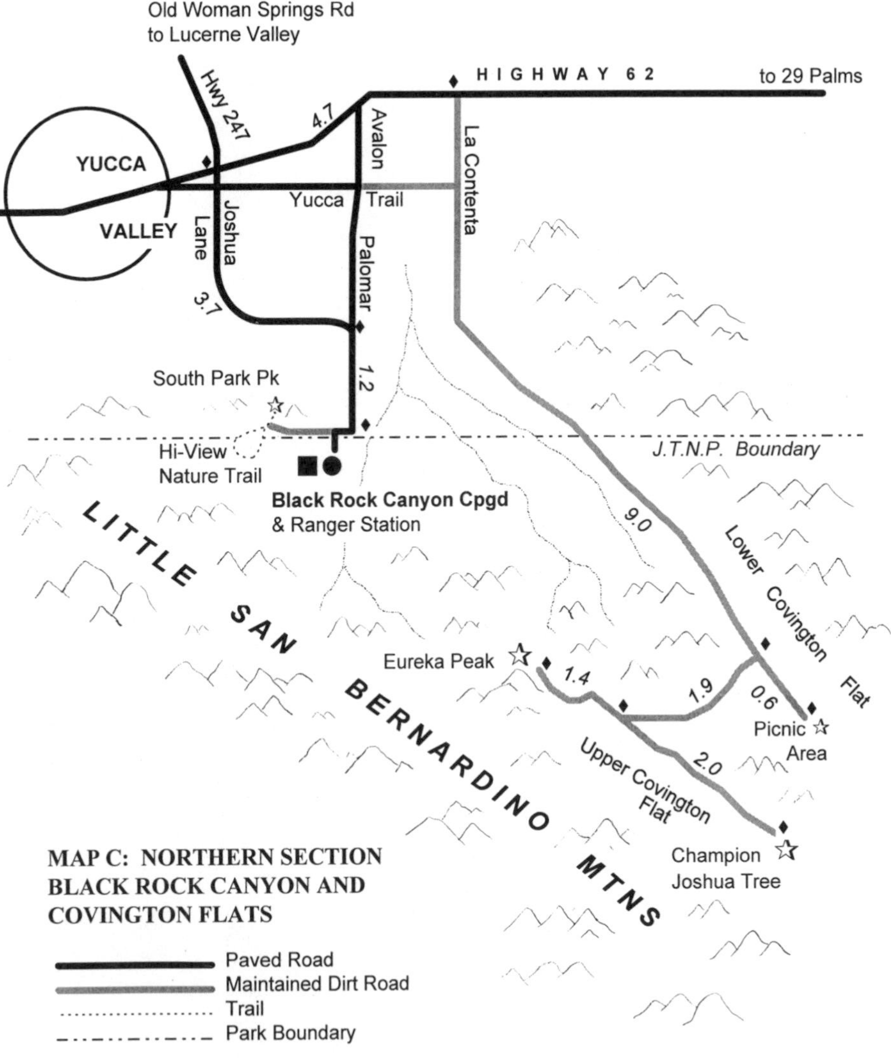

MAP C: NORTHERN SECTION BLACK ROCK CANYON AND COVINGTON FLATS

MAP D: NORTHERN SECTION
INDIAN COVE - TWENTYNINE PALMS

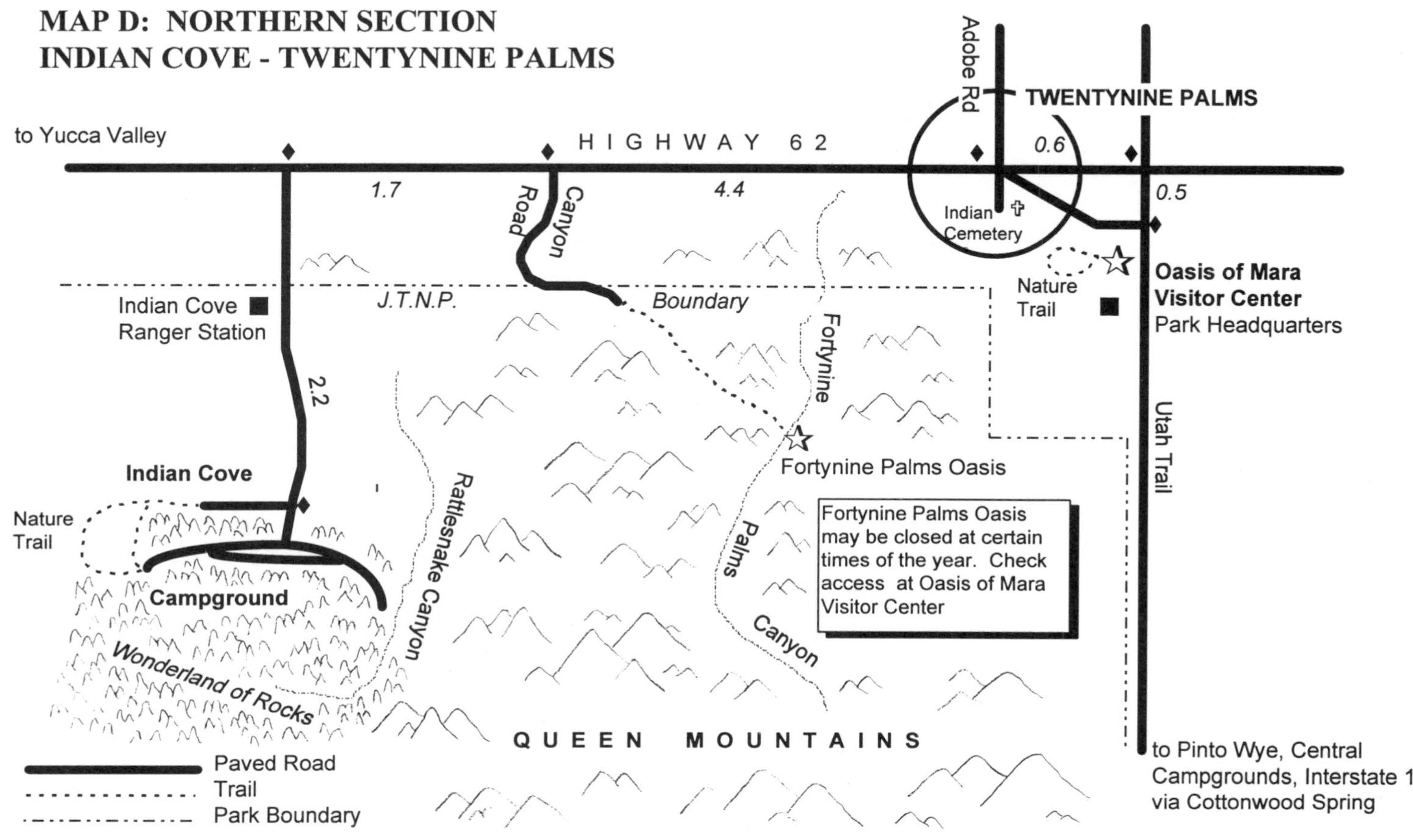

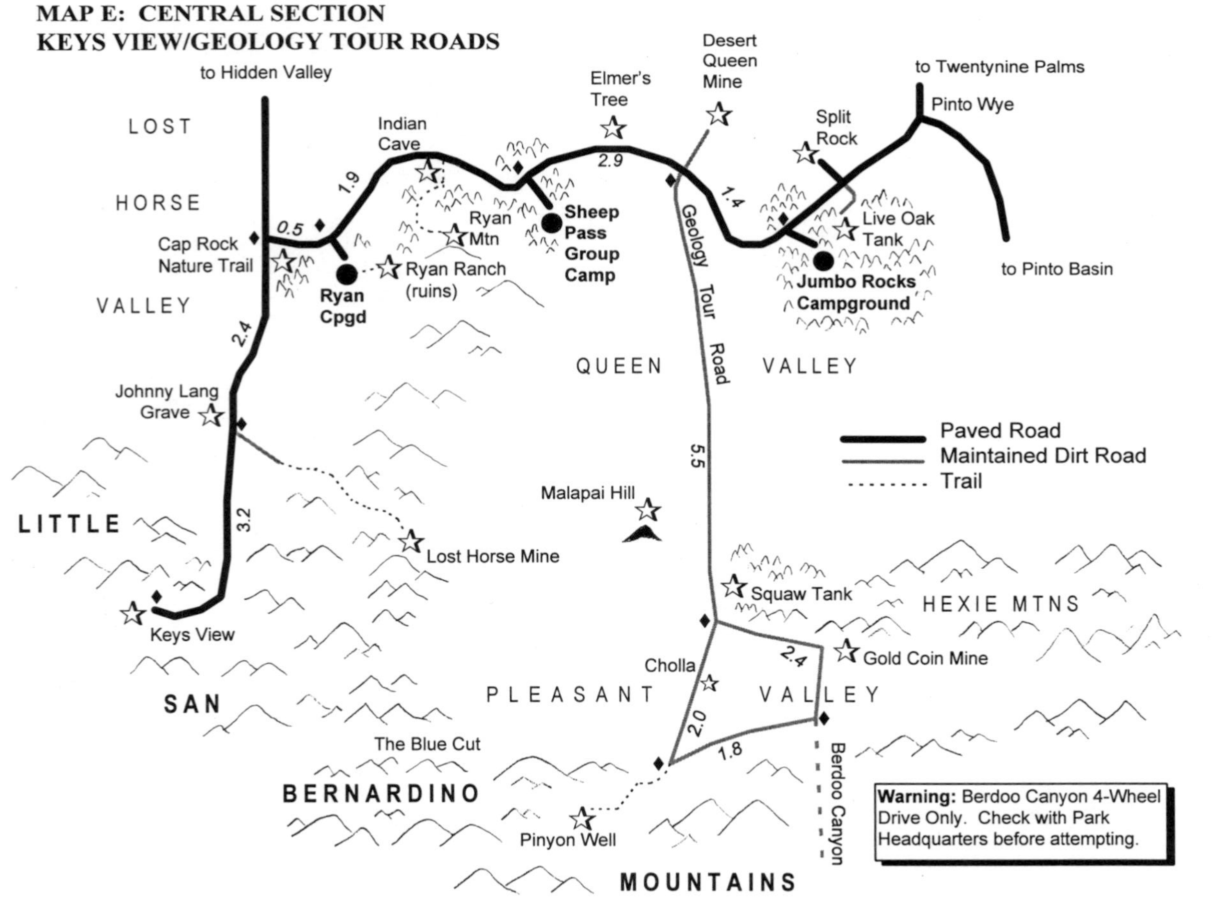
MAP E: CENTRAL SECTION
KEYS VIEW/GEOLOGY TOUR ROADS
to Hidden Valley
to Twentynine Palms
Pinto Wye
to Pinto Basin
LOST
HORSE
VALLEY
Cap Rock
Nature Trail
0.5
1.9
Indian
Cave
Ryan
Mtn
Ryan
Cpgd
Ryan Ranch
(ruins)
Sheep
Pass
Group
Camp
Elmer's
Tree
2.9
Desert
Queen
Mine
1.4
Split
Rock
Live Oak
Tank
Jumbo Rocks
Campground
Geology Tour Road
QUEEN
VALLEY
2.4
Johnny Lang
Grave
Paved Road
Maintained Dirt Road
Trail
5.5
Malapai Hill
LITTLE
3.2
Lost Horse Mine
Keys View
Squaw Tank
HEXIE MTNS
2.4
Gold Coin Mine
Cholla
SAN
PLEASANT
VALLEY
2.0
1.8
The Blue Cut
BERNARDINO
Berdoo Canyon
Warning: Berdoo Canyon 4-Wheel Drive Only. Check with Park Headquarters before attempting.
Pinyon Well
MOUNTAINS

The solitude, full of wild and weird mysteries, beckons to you
The mountains in their grim austerity call you.
The canyons in their studious secrecy whet your curiosity.
You must see; you must learn; you must know.
George Wharton James
Wonders of the Colorado Desert, 1906

CHAPTER 1

GETTING THE MOST FROM A VISIT

Joshua Tree National Park is more than a few groves of grotesque arborescent yuccas known as Joshua trees; it is a landscape of subtle surprises and charm. Like most desert places, it requires a little education in the ways of the desert to appreciate its underlying beauty; but the thread that weaves such bold, brilliant patterns in Yosemite and the Grand Canyon also runs true and unbroken in the fabric of Joshua Tree National Park.

To eyes unaccustomed to such wide-ranging landscapes, the California deserts may appear flat, monotonous and uninviting. What this arid land demands, and receives of its advocates, is a willingness to examine it on a closer, more intimate level. One may drive through a mountain forest never setting foot on the ground, yet still feel moved by the beauty of wilderness. But anyone who does not walk upon the desert, be it short strolls about the campground or long, arduous hikes, does not give the desert a fair chance to work its peculiar magic, to show one its hidden charms. Once captured by the desert 'wastelands', one comes to feel that Yosemite, Yellowstone, the Grand Canyon, and their near relatives are almost gaudy in their extravagant displays. Joshua Tree, too, has its embarrassment of riches, especially for those with discerning eyes.

The Visitor Centers

The quickest way to learn about Joshua Tree National Park is by means of the visitor centers.

The Oasis Visitor Center is located at Park Headquarters in Twentynine Palms on Utah Trail (the main road running south from Twentynine Palms into the park proper). Here are displays depicting early aboriginal habitation, desert flora and fauna, and man's interaction with the desert. Typical desert plants are cultivated on the grounds and labeled for easy identification. Adjacent to the Oasis Visitor Center is the Oasis of Mara, where a self-guiding trail wanders among cottonwood trees, mesquite thickets, and towering native palm trees.

The Cottonwood Visitor Center, located 7 miles north of Interstate 10 on the south entrance road, is a small facility that offers all the park publications for sale and has a useful, large scale map of the park on display. A naturalist is usually on duty.

Water

Water is not available in the park, but may be obtained at four peripheral sites - the Oasis Visitor Center at Twentynine Palms, Indian Cove Ranger Station adjacent to Indian Cove Campground, Black Rock Canyon Campground, and the Cottonwood Spring complex. Campers as well as day visitors should stock up with an adequate supply of fluids (up to a gallon per person a day in hot weather).

Gasoline, Accommodations and Food

Because of the absence of service facilities within the park, visitors should fill up their gasoline tanks before driving into the central part of the park. The winding roads cause higher consumption of gasoline than freeway driving.

There are no accommodations or dining facilities in the park. Lodging, gas, restaurants, and provisions are easily obtained in the communities of Yucca Valley, Joshua Tree, Twentynine Palms, Indio, Palm Springs, and Chiriaco Summit.

Growing up to 20 inches in length, the harmless chuckawalla inhabits most of the park campgrounds.

Camping

All campgrounds contain tables, fireplaces and toilets. The only campgrounds with water are Cottonwood and Black Rock Canyon. (Restrooms for the handicapped are located at several campgrounds; check with the visitor centers.) To keep the park in its natural condition, all vegetation, even that which is down and dead, is protected and cannot be used by campers. Visitors must bring their own firewood.

There are no electricity, water, or sewer connections for trailers. Camping is limited to 14 days between October 1st and June 1st, but is extended during the summer months to 30 days. Sites in the Sheep Pass, Indian Cove and Cottonwood Group Campgrounds may be reserved by organized groups. (No pickup campers, tent trailers, or R/V motor homes are allowed in group reservation sites.) At all other campgrounds individual campsites are available on a first-come basis; they are often filled to capacity on weekends in fall and spring.

CAMPGROUND	NUMBER OF SITES	ELEVATION (FT)	DESCRIPTION
Belle	20	3,800	Sites among rock formations
White Tank	20	3,800	Sites among rock formations
Jumbo Rocks	130	4,400	Sites among rock formations
Ryan	27	4,300	Open area near rock formations
Hidden Valley	62	4,200	Rock formations; rockclimbing area
Indian Cove	114	3,200	Sites in rocks at north edge of Wonderland of Rocks
Indian Cove Group	13	3,200	Organized group sites reserved by writing Park Headquarters
Sheep Pass Group	6	4,500	Reserved by writing; sites among rock formations
Cottonwood	62	3,000	Sites on open desert; flush toilets, water
Cottonwood Group	3	3,000	Reserved by writing
Black Rock Canyon	100	4,000	Mountainous area near Yucca Valley; flush toilets, water

Some campgrounds may charge fees. Check with Park Headquarters.

Weather

The deserts of the American Southwest are not always mercilessly bombarded by the sun and swept by scorching winds. Winter in Joshua Tree is a direct contrast to this stereotyped view, particularly in the western parts of the park where storms may deposit several inches of snow and hard overnight freezes are common.

As is the case over most of the Southwest, summer thunderstorms moving up from the south may bring more precipitation than westerly winter storms that have been forced to drop their liquid burdens on the coastal mountain barrier. The summer storms occur with greatest frequency in July and August, and although they can be extremely intense they rarely last for more than a few hours.

Because there is usually a 10 degree Fahrenheit temperature difference between the lower elevation areas, such as Twentynine Palms, and the high valleys of the central park, visitors can exercise a good deal of environmental control simply by moving into the higher elevations on warmer days and into the lower desert when cold weather predominates. To combat the energy-draining effects of the few really hot days, visitors can emulate the behavior of diurnal desert animals. They rise early to enjoy the coolness of morning, rest in the shade during midday, and resume activities in the late afternoon.

Listed below are average daily temperatures for Twentynine Palms (low desert) and Lost Horse Ranger Station (high desert near Hidden Valley Campground).

AVERAGE DAILY TEMPERATURES (Deg F)

	TWENTYNINE PALMS		LOST HORSE RANGER STN.	
	Min	Max	Min	Max
October	53.1	84.8	43.8	78.1
November	41.7	71.4	33.6	62.5
December	36.5	63.2	27.3	56.5
January	34.6	61.5	25.0	53.3
February	38.1	66.3	28.3	59.0
March	42.0	72.3	26.3	61.2
April	49.5	80.9	34.9	65.0
May	56.6	89.4	42.4	76.7
June	64.1	98.3	49.1	83.3
July	71.8	104.5	60.2	92.3
August	70.7	102.8	61.1	93.3
September	63.5	96.8	51.7	82.7

Wind

In a real blast there is little to do but take cover in a vehicle or structure. Winds are most likely to occur in the fall as part of the phenomenon known as the Santa Anas (or santanas), northeast winds that blow with unrelenting vigor sometimes for several days in succession. Usually their maximum strength occurs soon after dawn.

But the most violent winds are those that rush in from the coast during the winter, heralding the approach of rain. Lenticular clouds, shaped like flying saucers, blossom in the sky and hover over the mountains. Slowly more clouds gather and the rain falls. The harder the initial blow, the more chance for rain. Fortunately, these rain predictors are as rare as Southern California's rainstorms.

To give up and go home or to wait out the wind is always the question. On this point the author can give little advice. On several occasions when the howling gale seemed determined to blow forever, he has packed up and headed for home, only to have the furies abate and the day turn gloriously still. One never knows.

The most sheltered campgrounds are those where the sites are interspersed among giant boulders - Jumbo Rocks, White Tank, Indian Cove and Hidden Valley. The worst locations for wind are Cottonwood and Black Rock Canyon (although Black Rock partially compensates by having a large auditorium-ranger-station structure for shelter).

Visitor Services

Park Rangers conduct a wide variety of activities. These consist typically of nature walks, geology tours, hikes to abandoned mines and mill sites, rock-scrambling lessons, and the traditional evening campfire programs.

A unique feature at Joshua Tree National Park is the tour of the Desert Queen Ranch. Small groups are conducted on a walking tour of what was once a working ranch, now preserved as part of the park. The ranch buildings and equipment remain much as they were in their active past, serving to illustrate how man interacted with the desert environment, as well as demonstrating an independent way of life rapidly disappearing in

A scramble in the Wonderland of Rocks is just one of the many ranger-conducted activities offered by the Park Service.

today's complex world. Chapter 11 discusses the Desert Queen Ranch and its former owners.

A schedule of activities is posted at the visitor centers, at each campground, and at ranger stations throughout the park.

Spring Wildflowers

March, April and May are the best months to view the floral displays for which the desert is justly famous. The visitor centers can provide the latest information regarding the best wildflower viewing localities.

Driving

THERE ARE NO GAS STATIONS IN THE PARK; visitors should fill their fuel tanks before driving into the central regions.

Unless stated otherwise in this book, *all dirt roads should be suspect.* Inquire from park personnel before attempting to drive on them.

Users of off-road vehicles are cautioned that most of the park is designated as Wilderness Area wherein motorized travel of any kind is prohibited. Special motorcycle rules are posted around the park and are available at the visitor centers and ranger stations. *Vehicular traffic on other than established roads anywhere in the park is prohibited.* Visitors must also be careful to *park only in designated areas,* as destruction of desert vegetation by careless parking is subject to expensive fines.

Travel on foot can reveal unexpected delights such as these giant nolina plants.

Desert Walking

There are nine self-guiding interpretive trails and several other trails to points of interest in the park. The best way to gain an appreciation of the desert is to take these walks. Most are not strenuous and the trails are clearly marked.

Some hiking hints: (1) Note where you are going so you will remember how to return. Do this by memorizing landmarks, such as the shape of particular rocks or trees, and by glancing backwards. (2) Wear stout shoes (tennis shoes are usually adequate for the shorter nature trails). (3) Step carefully; what looks like firm rock underfoot sometimes consists of a deceptive layer of slippery, ball-bearing-like pebbles. (4) Examine the rocks and smell the plants; the desert is full of interesting textures and odors.

Unpleasant Creatures

Rattlesnakes, scorpions, tarantulas, centipedes and wasps are native inhabitants of Joshua Tree, but they are not nearly as common or as vicious as Hollywood would have us believe. The chance of encountering any of these animals is slight, and one is more likely to be struck by a lightning bolt than by a rattlesnake. On those rare occasions when rattlesnake bites are recorded, human misjudgment is usually at play. A teacher, who should have known better, picked up a rattlesnake in one of the campgrounds as part of a class demonstration, only to have the snake defend itself by the only means it could. Nevertheless, these creatures do exist (and in fact are protected in the park) so one should exercise proper caution even in the campgrounds. In particular, be aware of the placement of hands as well as feet when scrambling around boulders, since all these creatures take refuge in rocky crevices.

Clothing

Because of wide variations in temperature, it is best to wear layers of clothing that can be peeled off as the day warms up and replaced when temperatures drop. Even in winter the sun can be intense, so a hat and sunglasses can be most welcome. Finally, as previously mentioned, stout shoes or tennis shoes (as a minimum) are recommended. For hikes longer than the average nature trail, and especially for any off-trail walking, sturdy hiking boots are a must.

Special Equipment

Camera buffs may want to invest in a polarizing filter to enhance the blue skies and to obtain interesting contrast effects. A telephoto lens will be useful for photographing wildlife and rockclimbers in action. Joshua Tree National Park is a bird-lover's paradise, with at least 219 species having been sighted. To best enjoy this avian show, binoculars are a definite requirement.

Reference books dealing with plant and bird life are rewarding, but not if they are left at home. Some of the following books usually accompany the author in his car on trips to the desert:

A Field Guide to Pacific States Wildflowers, by Theodore F. Niehaus and Charles L. Ripper; Houghton Mifflin Company, Boston.

Desert Wildflowers, by Edmund C. Jaeger; Stanford University Press, Revised Edition.

California Desert Wildflowers, by Philip A. Munz; University of California Press.

California Spring Wildflowers, by Philip A. Munz; University of California Press.

The Native Cacti of California, by Lyman Benson; Stanford University Press.

Desert Tree Finder, by May Theilgaard Watts and Tom Watts; Nature Study Guild, Berkeley, California.

Field Guide to the Birds of North America, National Geographic Society, Washington, D.C..

Publications on all aspects of the park can be purchased at the Oasis of Mara Visitor Center.

Additional Information

Current information on all aspects of Joshua Tree National Park, including road conditions, reserving group campsites, and wildflower viewing locations, may be obtained by contacting Park Headquarters:

National Park Service
Joshua Tree National Park
74485 National Park Drive
Twentynine Palms, California 92277

Between these mountains and the mountains on the Mojave nothing is known of the country. I had never heard of a white man who had penetrated it. I am inclined to the belief that it is a barren, mountainous desert, composed of a system of basins and mountain ranges. It would be an exceedingly difficult country to explore, on account of the absence of water, and there is no rainy season of any consequence.

Lt. R.S. Williamson
Pacific Railroad Report, 1853

CHAPTER 2

THE IN-BETWEEN DESERT

Lieutenant Williamson was standing at the southern edge of present-day Joshua Tree National Park when he pondered the mysterious land beyond. Today the desert that aroused the Lieutenant's speculations is easily and safely explored by thousands of people every year. Yet this land of wide open spaces bounded by colorful but gaunt mountains still maintains, especially in the park where the hand of man has rested most lightly, a sense of the unknown that naturally draws out the exploring nature in people. Joshua Tree National Park is ideally suited to satisfy that urge. Its 1,236 square miles encompass all types of desert terrain - from sand dunes to deeply eroded canyons to pinyon-covered mountains. Furthermore, its location between two major deserts, the Mojave and the Sonoran, gives this "in-between desert" some of the characteristics of each, including the richest desert flora to be found in the state. In Joshua Tree National Park native palms rub shoulders with mountain-dwelling junipers, and cacti mix with Joshua tree forests, presenting an opportunity to explore and discover a unique environment.

The Mojave Desert

To the north of the park and penetrating into its western and central highlands is the Mojave Desert, a vast domain, yet the smallest and least complex of the four great deserts of North America. (The other three are the Chihuahuan, Great Basin, and Sonoran, of which the Sonoran is categorized into several subdivisions, the largest of which consists of the Colorado Desert.) The Mojave can be classified as "high desert", most of it lying between 3,000 and 5,000 feet above sea level. Winters can be severe, often accompanied by snowfall (usually at least once each season as far south as Joshua Tree National Park).

Creosote (*Larrea*) is the most common shrub of the Mojave, sometimes growing in pure stands many acres in extent but more often intermixed with a variety of other plant species. As omnipresent as the creosote may be, it surrenders the role as the true hallmark of the Mojave to another plant, the spindly Joshua tree. One way by which the boundaries of the Mojave Desert have been defined is by the distribution of this strange plant. In an otherwise treeless desert, the Joshua tree has become a dominant and essential ecological element of the landscape. Only the Mojave yucca (*Yucca schidigera*) and the nolina (*Nolina bigelovii*) approach the Joshua tree in size and distribution, but they never attain the same towering stature.

Mountain ranges dot the Mojave Desert like misplaced ocean archipelagos, and constitute an important aspect of Joshua Tree National Park. The island analogy is a good one, for being at higher elevations than the surrounding desert these far flung ranges receive more moisture and support a different plant community than the surrounding ocean of arid plains and valleys. The mountain plant community is dominated by pinyon pines and junipers, an open woodland that occurs throughout the higher parts of the park (above 4,000 feet) often in conjunction with the Joshua tree forests.

The Colorado Desert

Approaching from the south and blending into the Mojave Desert in Joshua Tree National Park is the Colorado Desert. This largest subdivision of the greater Sonoran Desert is characteristically low-lying in elevation (less than 3,000 feet) and considerably hotter and drier on the average than the Mojave Desert. One would expect it to be bleaker, too, yet the Colorado Desert, like the Sonoran as a whole, is botanically rich, much more so than the Mojave. Whereas few cacti have adapted to withstand the rigors of Mojavean winters, an impressive array of these succulent plants thrive in the Colorado Desert where freezes are exceptionally rare. Unlike the Mojave Desert with its single species of tree, the Colorado Desert, homeland of the mesquite, smoke tree, palo verde, ironwood, and that 'Prince of Vegetables', the native palm, presents a comparatively tree-rich environment.

Two conspicuous plant species that serve as indicators of the Colorado Desert are the ocotillo (*Fouquieria splendens*) and the viciously-armed Bigelow or Teddy-bear cholla (*Opuntia bigelovii*). Prominent stands of these plants are located along the road in Pinto Basin. (The Ocotillo Patch and the Cholla Garden are described in more detail in Chapter 19.) Probably no other cactus on the desert has a more well-deserved fearsome reputation for its spines than 'Bigelow's Accursed Cholla'.

The In-Between Desert of Joshua Tree National Park

Strategically located between two different desert domains, with its great variety of terrain and elevation, Joshua Tree offers the visitor a unique laboratory for observing a host of fascinating desert plants.

The most striking example of the strange patterns of plant distribution arising from the in-between location of the park occurs in the Eagle Mountains near Cottonwood Spring. Here in the rugged upper reaches of Munsen Canyon at a lofty elevation of 4,500 feet, native palm trees, a species normally associated with the low-lying Colorado Desert, are found growing beside high-country junipers, plants more at home on the mountaintops of the Mojave Desert.

Elsewhere in the park, where soil and climatic conditions are exactly right a particular plant species may attain local dominance. The aforementioned Ocotillo Patch and Cholla Garden are not the only examples. Myriads of hedgehog cactus (*Echinocereus engelmannii*) crowd around the eastern base of Malapai Hill, while the nearby south-facing slopes of the Hexie Mountains bordering Pleasant Valley support an extravagant display of barrel cactus (*Ferocactus acanthodes*). In another area within Pleasant Valley, diamond cholla (*Opuntia ramosissima*) predominate and assume gigantic proportions. (See Chapter 15 regarding the Pleasant Valley/Malapai Hill region.)

The more one explores Joshua Tree, the more variety one discovers. The park's unique location between the Mojave and Colorado deserts accounts for the great abundance of plant species. Thanks to the efforts of a few far-sighted individuals, this great laboratory has been preserved for all of us to explore, enjoy, and appreciate.

I once asked an old Colorado Desert prospector how many varieties of cactus he was familiar with. "By gosh," said he, "you city fellers have no idea how many kinds we got. I know every one of 'em. There's the 'full of stickers,' 'all stickers,' 'never-fail stickers,' 'stick everybody,' 'the stick and stay in,' 'the sharp stickers,' 'the extra sharp stickers,' 'big stickers,' 'little stickers,' 'big and little stickers,' 'stick while you sleep,' 'stick while you wait,' 'stick 'em alive,' 'stick 'em dead,' 'stick unexpectedly,' 'stick anyhow,' 'stick through leather,' 'stick through anything,' 'the stick in and never come out,' 'the stick and fester cactus,' 'the cat's claws cactus,' 'the barbed fish-hook cactus,' 'the rattlesnake's fang cactus,' 'the stick seven ways at once cactus,' 'the impartial sticker,' 'the democratic sticker,' 'the deep sticker,' and a few others."

George Wharton James

Wonders of the Colorado Desert, 1906

No one who heard her talk could ever again regard the subject of conservation of desert flora with indifference.

Anonymous

CHAPTER 3

MRS. HOYT'S MONUMENT

Minerva Hamilton Hoyt was a large and stately woman, aristocratic and wealthy, and deeply involved with all the socially correct charitable organizations of 1900s Los Angeles and Pasadena. She was what one might refer to as a 'society matron'. She most certainly was not a sun-hardened desert rat. But something in the open spaces and comforting solitude of the California desert stirred her soul, with the result that she almost single-handedly led the crusade to create Joshua Tree National Monument, the predecessor to the National Park.

Joshua Tree is just one of a multitude of superb parks and monuments that we Americans tend to take for granted. But parks do not simply spring into existence, and in taking them for granted, we ignore the efforts and sacrifices of those who labor so diligently to create these havens of wild beauty. The story of Minerva Hoyt and her legacy deserves telling not just for history's sake, but as an example of how conservationists have always and still continue to function - largely upon the storehouse of their own hopes and inspiration.

At the beginning of the twentieth century the California desert was a place to be avoided unless you were a hermit or one of the few hardy miners bent on hunting and digging for mineral wealth. The popular conception of the desert was that it was always hot, uncomfortable, and dangerous - and it could indeed be all these things. Travel to the desert and across its vast expanses was a difficult undertaking. But by the 1920s a change was taking place, a change that created far-reaching problems for the desert that have yet to be satisfactorily resolved.

It was the automobile revolution, and with it came the discovery that the wagon roads developed by teamsters hauling freight to isolated desert sites could be negotiated by the tin lizzie. Ever-increasing numbers of tourists came pouring out of the coastal metropolitan areas of Southern California into a new-found playground where the air was pure and the sky nearly always clear.

What began to trouble Mrs. Hoyt and others was not the mere presence of greater numbers of people on the desert - its vastness was capable of absorbing the new multitudes unnoticed - but the increasing incidence of vandalism in the form of wholesale uprooting of native desert vegetation to be transplanted to city-dwellers' gardens. With the recreational discovery of the desert during the

1920s, cactus gardens seemed to suddenly sprout around every home and bungalow in Southern California. As time went on, the problem grew to epidemic proportions. Fully-grown palm trees were being removed from native oases to grace urban patios. Far worse was the decimation of the Devil's Garden, the sparse remains of which are still visible along the first five miles of Highway 62 after it branches from Interstate 10 north of Palm Springs. Here once was located the epitome of Colorado Desert plant life, thousands of acres containing the most concentrated congregation of yuccas and cacti on all the California desert. George Wharton James described the site in his book, *Wonders of the Colorado Desert* (1906): "When we find ourselves on the mesa we begin to understand why this is called by the prospectors 'the devil's garden.' It is simply a vast, native, forcing ground for a thousand varieties of cactus. They thrive here as if specially guarded....I know of no place where so many varieties are to be found as in this small area near the Morongo Pass." By 1930 it had been stripped bare, to the extent that even now, after decades of recovery, the passing motorist barely notices the sparse covering of cacti that has slowly reclaimed the area.

The Devil's Garden (1906)

Just as exasperating was the vandalism directed toward the Joshua tree. Travellers crossing the desert at night were setting fire to individual Joshua trees to guide other motorists. Then on June 14, 1930, the tallest Joshua tree ever known to exist was put to the torch and killed by unknown vandals.

The job of obtaining protection for the "worthless" desert was a long one (and in fact continues to this day). Mrs. Hoyt realized that her first task would be one of educating the public and government to appreciate desert values. In the late 1920s she initiated the process by mounting a series of highly acclaimed desert exhibitions, consisting of realistic habitat displays, in the United States and England, winning the support of influential scientists and the backing of the country's many garden clubs. In 1930 the next stage in her campaign evolved with her formation of the International Deserts Conservation League, created "...to respond to an urgent demand for the protection of desert life and conservation of desert beauty spots."

Shortly thereafter Mrs. Hoyt first publicly broached the idea of a large federal desert park, to encompass over 1,000,000 acres located roughly where Joshua Tree National Monument came to be established, but stretching eastward all the way to the Colorado River. Horace M. Albright, then Director of the National Park Service, was sympathetic, but due to the pressing tasks facing his overworked agency in establishing two other desert projects (Saguaro National Monument in Arizona and Death Valley National Monument in California), he felt he could not commit Park Service resources for a third desert effort. Albright also recognized that a checkerboard pattern of land ownership within Mrs. Hoyt's proposed park boundaries (a Southern Pacific Railroad land grant consisting of every other section of land extended over much of the area), combined with a scattering of homesteads and mining claims, presented additional complications.

Despite this disappointment, Mrs. Hoyt remained convinced that a federal desert park was required. In 1933 a bill was passed in the California legislature to create a "California Desert Park" that would have encompassed much of the area in Mrs. Hoyt's proposal. In response to this threat to her federal project, Mrs. Hoyt asked Governor Rolph to give her more time to plead her case before the federal government. Rolph cooperated, not only vetoing the state bill, but also presenting Mrs. Hoyt with a letter of introduction to newly-elected President Franklin D. Roosevelt. In the subsequent meeting with Roosevelt and Secretary of the Interior Harold Ickes she was buoyed by their receptivity to her proposal. Ickes summed it up: "The President is for this and I am for this."

Now Mrs. Hoyt drew upon the expertise of two eminent scientists, Drs. Philip Munz and Edmund C. Jaeger, to compile a two-volume photographic and written description of the outstanding plants, scenery, and recreational attractions of the area under proposal. This resource survey served as the basis for the establishment of Joshua Tree National Monument.

Neither Ickes nor Roosevelt was intimidated by the private property problems associated with the project. Four months after Hoyt's meeting with them, an area of 1,136,000 acres was withdrawn for consideration as a new national park or monument.

Success for Mrs. Hoyt? Not yet. During the next three years she tirelessly conducted official tours of the area, while simultaneously cajoling, badgering, and generally lobbying government officials to formally establish a national monument of maximum size. Finally, on August 10, 1936, President Roosevelt signed the proclamation setting aside 825,000 acres of prime California desert as Joshua Tree National Monument.

Minerva Hoyt, who has been referred to as the "Apostle of the Cacti" due to her unflagging devotion to desert preservation, died in 1945. Through her self-sacrifice, you and I, and all the people who visit this part of California, have the opportunity to scramble over the gigantic boulders in the Wonderland of Rocks, explore the scenic Joshua tree forests, wonder at the vastness of Pinto Basin, or trek into the backcountry where the clever hand of man has not wreaked its typical havoc.

Threats, Compromise and Boundary Adjustments

The efforts of conservationists are rarely appreciated in their own time. The arguments of Hoyt, Munz, and Jaeger, the official proclamations of Ickes and Roosevelt, expressing the desire of the people to save a unique area of the California desert from the forces of exploitation and destruction, were anathema to one important Western industry.

A belt of moderate mineralization was known to exist in the northeast and eastern portions of the new national monument. The mines of the Dale and Gold Park districts north of Pinto Basin had been worked off and on since the 1880s, and although a few of them had met with slight success, the high cost of freighting and the problems of obtaining water made most mines a marginal operation at best. By 1936 when the monument was established, most of the profitable mineral deposits had been thoroughly depleted, but to this day prospectors continue to find "color" in the rough hills of Dale.

Farther south, in the Eagle Mountains, Kaiser Steel had an interest in a large iron ore deposit which it protected by patenting its claims prior to the establishment of the national monument. In fact the several thousand existing claims within the new monument were to remain valid; only the establishment of new mining ventures was prohibited.

Miners are eternal optimists. The next bonanza is always just under the next rock or over the next hill, no matter how many times the territory has been probed, worked over, and rejected. Therefore the restriction on new claims was bitterly opposed. Pressure formed to open the monument to unrestricted mining, or better yet, to do away with the monument altogether. So successful were the mining interests that conservation groups felt it necessary to offer a compromise rather than risk losing the entire area. The resultant Phillips Bill, enacted in 1950, transferred 289,000 acres of the original monument, including the known mineral belt, back into the public domain, in return for which funds were provided to acquire private inholdings within the remaining monument.

Still the miners were not satisfied. In 1951 the Western Mining Council passed a resolution asking the government to open up the monument. And again, in 1954, conservation groups were forced to rally to stop the mining interests from obtaining a similar resolution from the San Bernardino County Board of Supervisors.

Under this constant threat of exploitation, the Desert Protective Council was formed in the latter part of 1954. Following in the footsteps of Minerva Hoyt's long-defunct International Deserts Conservation League, the new organization's purpose was and remains "...to safeguard for wise and reverent use by this and succeeding generations those desert areas that are of unique scenic, scientific, historical, spriritual, and recreational values." Thanks to the efforts of the Desert Protective Council, and sibling environmental organizations such as the Sierra Club, National Audubon Society and the Wilderness Society, Joshua Tree remained in the hands of all the people of the United States under the stewardship of the National Park Service.

From National Monument to National Park

In addition to changing the status of Joshua Tree from national monument to national park, the California Desert Protection Act of 1994 added 243,000 acres of near-pristine desert to the park. Much of the new acreage was added on the east, completing ecological units in the Coxcomb Mountains and Eagle Mountains. Another large unit was added along the southwestern edge to bring the boundary down to the Los Angeles aqueduct road. The new areas are mostly roadless and present near-pristine wilderness for the desert hiker. Of great importance will be the added protection given to wildlife resources, particularly the desert tortoise and desert bighorn sheep. We must again acknowledge the hard work of those environmentalists who worked to preserve and pass down the treasure that is Joshua Tree National Park.

As a last comment, the author acknowledges the value of old mining ruins. They are picturesque and add a touch of human interest as reminders of an earlier and important historical era. But a drive through the old Dale District reveals what the park might have become if it had been "opened up." Dale has its interesting ruins, but there is trash wherever the miners cared to leave it and, of course, the inevitable "no trespassing" signs on numberless semi-active claim sites. You are encouraged to walk up to an old mill or mine site in Joshua Tree National Park; one can't be as casual in Dale.

On the cover of the current issue of the California Mining Journal is the picture of Joshua trees, with the following caption: "The Joshua Trees of San Bernardino and Riverside counties - eight hundred acres of them block the mining industry in that area! This vast acreage has been withdrawn from public entry to protect a few scrubby trees that are of absolutely no value - sentimental or otherwise."

Desert Magazine, April, 1946

*A more detailed account of Mrs. Hoyt's activities is recounted in an article, *"Apostle of the Cacti": The Society Matron as Environmental Activist*, by Conner Sorensen, appearing in the *Southern California Quarterly*, Vol. LVIII, No. 3, Fall 1976.

We were struck by the appearance of yucca trees, which gave a strange and southern character to the country and suited well with the dry and desert region we were approaching. Associated with the idea of barren sands, their stiff and ungraceful forms makes them to the traveller the most repulsive tree in the vegetable kingdom.

John C. Fremont, 1844

CHAPTER 4

ORANGES ON JOSHUA TREES

Captain Fremont was not alone in his opinion of the arborescent tree yucca we call the Joshua tree. Some 80 years later, mild-mannered J. Smeaton Chase, a desert lover if ever there was one, recorded an even more extreme reaction in his book *California Desert Trails* (1919):

> It is a weird, menacing object, more like some conception of Poe's or Dore's than any work of wholesome Mother Nature. One can scarcely find a term of ugliness that is not apt for this plant. A misshapen pirate with belt, boots, hands, and teeth stuck full of daggers is as near as I can come to a human analogy. The wood is a harsh, rasping fibre; knife-blades, long, hard, and keen, fill the place of leaves; the flower is greenish white and ill-smelling; and the fruit a cluster of nubbly pods, bitter and useless. A landscape filled with Joshua trees has a nightmare effect even in broad daylight; at the witching hour it can be almost infernal.

But the "misshapen pirate" has had friends, as well. William Manly, struggling out of Death Valley to seek help for a marooned party of 1849'ers, called the Joshua "a brave little tree to live in such barren country."

It is the Mormons, if legends be true, who derived great inspiration from this awkward plant, and in doing so gave us its common name. There are many versions to the story, but Dennis H. Stovall, writing in the September 1938 issue of *Desert Magazine,* claims to have discovered the specific incident leading to the naming of the Joshua tree. According to Stovall, a band of Mormon colonists under the leadership of Elisha Hunt, in the year 1851, was crossing the Mojave Desert enroute from Utah to San Bernardino, California. A hot sun, foretelling the approach of summer, shimmered overhead, draining the energy of humans and animals alike. As if by a miracle a cloud rolled in front of the sun, just as the party approached a Joshua tree forest. The leader exclaimed, "Look brethren! The sky is no longer like brazen brass. God has sent the clouds. It is as if the sun stood still

- as Joshua commanded. These green trees are lifting their arms to heaven in supplication. We shall call them Joshua trees!"

(Note: the Spanish and Mexican explorers who first penetrated the great deserts of the Southwest referred to Joshua trees as 'cabbage palms'. The first American description of the tree yucca consists of a journal entry made by Jedediah Smith on his epic pioneer march across the Mojave Desert in 1827. He named it the 'dirk Pear tree' because in size and shape it resembles the pear tree but with leaves like the 'blade of a dirk'.)

Growth Patterns

Even in an exotic jungle setting the Joshua tree would stand out as an oddity, if only because of its unusual shape. Branches thrust out in every conceivable direction. Many of these desert trees seem to deliberately adopt the most awkward pose possible. Dangling, dead limbs often add a final grotesque touch. A few individuals display perfect crowns of many-branched limbs each terminated by a cluster of dark green, dagger-like leaves. The effect can be startlingly beautiful, as with the largest Joshua tree in the park, towering supremely over a court of giants in Upper Covington Flat. Other magnificent specimens raise their shaggy heads beside the park highway in Queen Valley (refer to Chapter 15).

It is the short, stiff, sharply pointed leaves that give the Joshua tree its botanical name *Yucca brevifolia* - the short-leafed yucca. The leaves develop at the ends of the limbs in the terminal bud where all new growth takes place. As the limb continues growing, the older leaves die and cling to the branch, forming a shag that eventually drops off to expose the rough bark beneath.

The prime characteristic of the Joshua tree is its many branchings. Every young plant begins growing in a straight, upright column. These good soldiers soon rebel and begin branching, not on their own initiative, but in response to either of two events that may occur to the terminal bud; a flower bud develops, or the terminal bud suffers physical damage from insects or the elements. Either way, new leaf formation is halted. To continue growing, the column forks just below the old bud into two or more limbs, each complete with a new, healthy terminal bud. The process may be repeated many times in the life of the plant, and since blooming or insect damage does not occur in each branch simultaneously, some limbs develop longer segments than others, thus accounting for the Joshua tree's unpredictable form.

An entertaining game to pursue while passing through the Joshua tree forests (on foot is best, but it can be played from a car window as well) is to look for especially large or strangely shaped individuals - one often recognizes a tall, lanky relative or acquaintance. One oddity discovered by Dr. Edmund Jaeger was a Joshua tree that had shot straight up for 22 feet before dividing into four short branches. A pair of enterprising red-tailed hawks had constructed a nest in this natural cradle atop the tree.

Perhaps Captain Fremont's disdain for the Joshua tree originated when he stopped to sniff one of the curious blossoms. The creamy white flowers occur in a cluster, or panicle, at the ends of branches, looking like an odd cross between a cauliflower and an artichoke. They possess a musty, slightly malodorous odor, but one must literally bury one's nose in a blossom to experience it. The flowering season usually commences in March, and by May the branch tips may be heavily laden with light green seed pods resembling big pecan shells.

In addition to reproducing by seeds, the Joshua tree sends out long, bamboo-like runners. Most of the smaller Joshuas near a larger specimen will have originated by this technique. Except for the runners, most of the tree's roots are no larger in diameter than a pencil. They form a large clump around the base of the trunk, making a very effective anchor against strong desert winds.

Age and Distribution

How old are Joshua trees? No sure method of age determination has been developed. A large tree's grizzled exterior gives an appearance of great age; in a dense forest one feels thrust back to a primordial era. Early references claim Joshua trees live over a thousand years. One problem with the Joshua tree is that although arborescent or treelike in form, it is not really a "tree" in the usual sense of the word. It is closely related to the lilies and agaves, or century plants, and while its pithy core does produce growth rings, there is controversy over whether they represent annual rings in the manner of common oaks, pines and elms. Core sampling, a method for obtaining annual growth ring data for ordinary trees, is difficult and often impossible to perform on Joshua trees. Not only is the wood quite soft, but the centers of larger Joshuas often decay, leaving air-filled voids.

Probably the best method for estimating age is based on the assumption of an average growth rate. Over a period of years the growth of several trees in the park was monitored and a resultant average growth rate of 1.5 centimeters per year was determined. Thus a thousand-year-old tree would presumably measure approximately 15 meters (over 45 feet) in height. No such giants are found in the park, but a number of trees surely are in the 700 to 800 year age bracket.

Because it has appeared as scenic backdrops in so many Hollywood films, the Joshua tree has become an emblem of the American desert. It actually inhabits only the Mojave Desert, reaching its southernmost limit in Joshua Tree National Park. In fact *Yucca brevifolia* is so closely associated with the Mojave that scientists often use its distribution to delineate the boundaries of that desert.

It is hard to imagine that the tough, fibrous, dagger-pointed leaves of the Joshua tree could be a tasty morsel for any beast, yet there was one large animal that grazed on the Joshua tree forests, and in so doing presented us with information about the past history of the Mojave Desert. In the late 1940s, caves were discovered in eastern Nevada containing the preserved dung of *Nothrotherium*, an extinct ground sloth that roamed the Southwest as late as 15,000 years ago. Analysis revealed that a major constituent of the ground sloth's diet was the Joshua tree. The caves are located far to the east of the present limit of Joshua tree growth, so apparently the Joshua tree, and by inference the Mojave Desert, occupied a larger area in the past.

In Joshua Tree National Park the Joshua trees are found at higher elevations, usually above 3500 feet, where precipitation is greater than adjacent low-lying parts of the Colorado Desert. At these elevations winter freezes often occur and there is usually at least one good snow storm per season. The hardy Joshua tree seems to thrive only where it can experience this extreme climate. Nor is it particularly attracted to water, preferring the well-drained alluvium surrounding decomposing mountains. Where conditions are right, great forests of Joshua trees proliferate, such as in Lost Horse and Queen valleys. A grove of spectacular giant Joshua trees is located in Upper Covington Flat in the northwest corner of the park (see Chapter 8).

A Tree of Life

In the vast shrub-land of the Mojave Desert, the Joshua tree has assumed a dominant ecological role. This is most clearly demonstrated by the number and diversity of animals that have come to depend on or in some way make use of the Joshua tree.

At least 25 species of birds are known to use the tree yucca as a nesting site. Woodpeckers bore into the limbs, creating dens that are often used by other birds. Considerable engineering ability is demonstrated by Scott's oriole, whose cleverly designed domiciles are woven from dead yucca leaves and suspended like hammocks between the bristling Joshua branches.

Birds of prey use the Joshua trees for observation posts as well as nesting sites. A drive through a Joshua tree forest, especially in the early morning hours, will inevitably reveal a hawk perched on the topmost branch of a roadside Joshua tree, apparently oblivious to the automobile traffic until someone stops to take a closer look.

The loggerhead shrike, a carnivorous bird resembling the common mockingbird in both size and coloration, puts the dagger-like leaves of *Yucca brevifolia* to good use. Swooping from tree top to tree top on its hunting rounds, the shrike occasionally touches the ground and carries away a wriggling lizard. The loggerhead's more common appellation - butcherbird - is explained by its habit of skewering the remains of its prey on one of the sharp yucca leaves, hanging its meat like a butcher, perhaps to return to it later in the day.

A mammal making extensive use of the Joshua tree is the woodrat (*Neotoma*). The unmistakable signs of a woodrat at work are Joshua tree limbs from which the leaves have been neatly and uniformly trimmed close to the trunk. Nearby, perhaps around the base of another Joshua tree, will be found the pile of rubble - sticks, brush, cactus joints, and, of course, the missing Joshua tree leaves - that comprise the nest of this solitary and industrious little creature.

Who was here? Woodrat at left, yucca boring weevil at right.

Insects play an important role in the life of the Joshua tree. Foremost in causing damage to the Joshua tree's terminal bud, and thus contributing to the tree's many branchings, is the yucca boring weevil (*Scyphophorus yuccae*). The larvae, issuing from eggs laid in the terminal bud, devour the surrounding plant tissue and build tough frass cases from which they emerge as adult beetles. In response to this damage, the tree exudes silica from the adjacent tissue, creating the so-called "petrified" Joshua tree wood that remains after a dead tree has completely decayed. Joshua tree limbs that have a "coolie hat" appearance at their tips formed by dead, turned-back leaves are most likely infested by this insect.

A butterfly known as the Navaho yucca borer (*Megathymus yuccae navaho*) propagates itself by laying its eggs on juvenile Joshua trees; but not just any young plant will do. Those tree yuccas that have grown from seeds will not provide an adequate food supply for the rapacious larvae. Only by penetrating into the large runners sent out by a parent tree can the larvae mature and pupate. In some mysterious way the female yucca borer is able to differentiate between the sprouts that have germinated from seeds and those that have grown from runners, and lays her eggs only on the latter. The resulting infestation and severing of the resource draining offshoots probably benefits the parent plant.

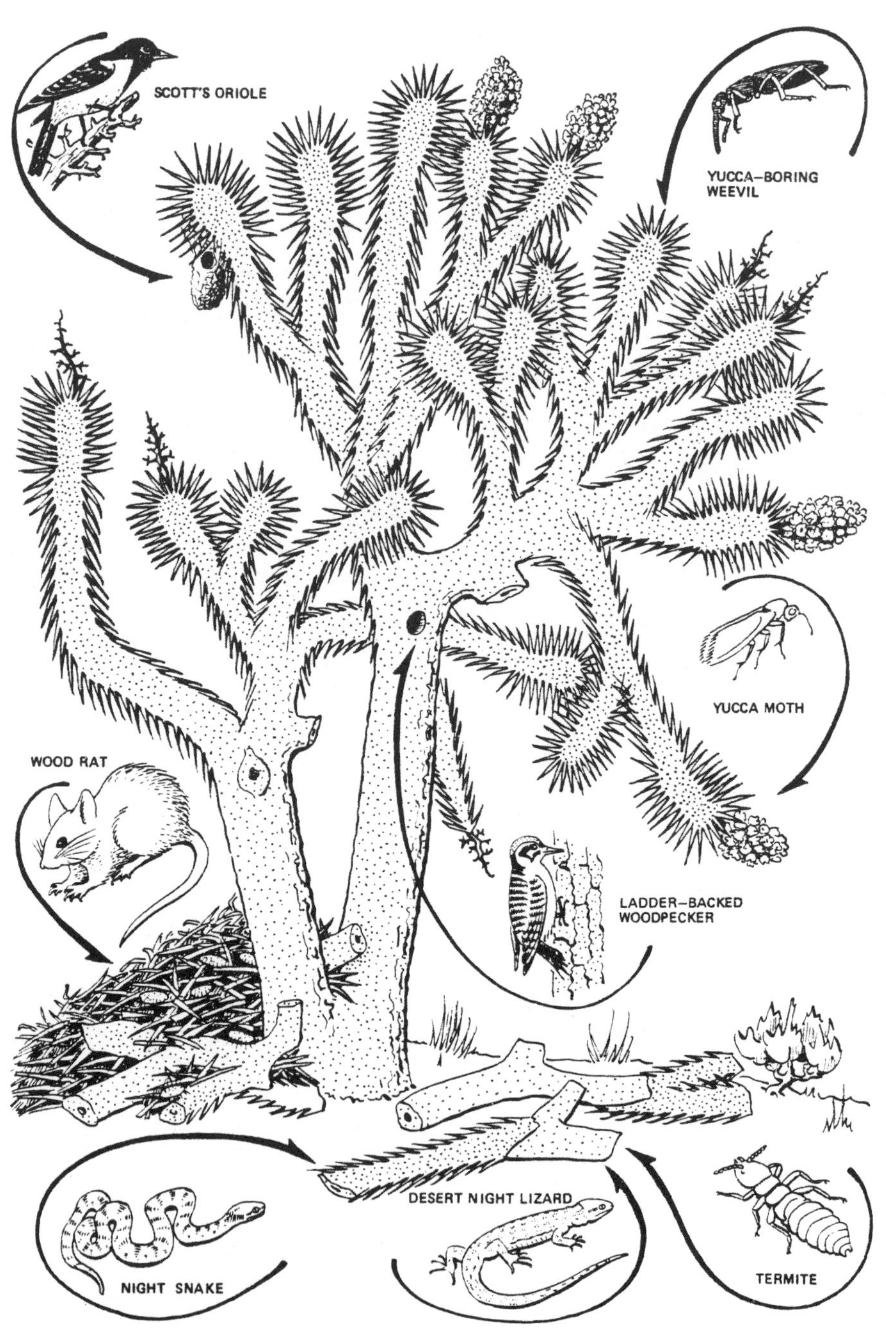

Drawing from *An Island Called California*, by Elna Bakker; University of California Press, 1971.

A marvelous example of the evolutionary development of interdependent living forms presents itself in the strange and beautiful relationship between the Joshua tree and the yucca moth, *Pronuba synthetica.* The story begins many thousands of years ago when the ancestral yucca plant evolved the characteristic of having sticky pollen, as opposed to cone-bearing trees which have a dry, dusty pollen that is freely blown from tree to tree. As this occurred, the *Pronuba* species of moth stumbled upon a method by which it could ensure its survival, and in pursuing that method both moths and yuccas turned onto an evolutionary pathway that eventually made them dependent upon each other. What the ancestral *Pronuba* moth 'learned' was to gather yucca pollen with which to deliberately fertilize the yucca flower and then lay its eggs in the soon-to-develop yucca ovary. The growing seeds thus serve as a guaranteed food source for the young larvae. The moth never lays so many eggs that all the yucca seeds will be devoured; some always survive to ensure propagation of new yuccas which in turn serve future generations of yucca moths.

As a result of the yucca moth's activities, those yuccas with flowers most attractive to the moth, i.e., with sticky pollen that was easier for the moth to manipulate, stood greater chances of being visited and of producing seeds. Thus the yuccas slowly lost the ability to be pollinated by any other method than that offered by the moth. The whole process probably took many thousands of years, and as different species of yuccas evolved, so did different species of *Pronuba.*

Another remarkable insect enters into the *Pronuba*-Joshua tree relationship. A small, dark-brown *Ichneumon* wasp, if noticed at all while it buzzes around the clusters of yucca seed pods, seems most unnoteworthy. But if watched closely, it will be observed to be conducting a careful search. At last it alights, inserts its ovipositor through the tough green skin of the yucca fruit and deposits a solitary egg. Examination reveals that the wasp has invariably located one of the larvae of the *Pronuba* moth, which it has paralyzed to serve as food for the wasp larva that will soon hatch from the deposited egg. How the little wasp detects the deeply buried *Pronuba* moth larva is another desert mystery.

Even in death the Joshua tree is a source of life. Termites inhabit downed limbs and dead stumps, returning basic nutrients to the soil. Along with other insects, they fall prey to another resident of dead Joshua trees, the yucca night lizard, *Xantusia vigilis.* Insects, lizards, packrats: these in turn provide sustenance for birds and bats, snakes and other carnivores. When we learn of the full implication of the Joshua tree and its complex ecology, we cannot help but develop a great appreciation for this strange and wonderful symbol of the Mojave Desert.

The Joshua Tree and Man

Man as well as beast has discovered uses for the humble Joshua tree. The Indians found the tree to be both a source of food and of raw material for manufactured goods. The massive flower buds were eaten raw or roasted. Later in the season, seed pods continued to provide nourishment. The coarse fibers from the leaves were used in making sandals and carrying nets. Smaller roots of the Joshua tree yielded red strands useful in basketry as well as a red dye. An unfading black fiber was obtained by maintaining a slow-burning fire for three days over the buried roots. The roots also produced a sudsy concoction used either as a shampoo or taken internally as a laxative.

The white man in his usual cleverness has exploited the Joshua tree in a more severe manner than the Indians. Pioneers used tree trunks and limbs in the construction of corrals and fences. In the dry desert climate the dead fibrous wood becomes resistant to decay. An example of this use may be seen at the Desert Queen Ranch (Chapter 11), where long-standing fences, corrals and massive gate posts attest to the durability of this building material.

Pioneer homesteader Bill Keys stands beside corral he constructed from Joshua tree logs at the Desert Queen Ranch. (photo by Fred Mang, National Park Service)

Considering some of the schemes devised by man to exploit the Joshua tree, we are lucky to have them around at all. There was, for example, the great Joshua tree paper-making enterprise. This episode transpired in the 1880s when the Atlantic and Pacific Fiber Company, of London, England, acquired 5,200 acres of Joshua tree land near Palmdale, California, for the purpose of providing Joshua tree paper to the London Daily Telegraph. (Palmdale was not named for the presence of native palm trees, which do not range that far north, but for the locally abundant Joshua trees which were called "palms" by the early explorers and settlers.) A crew of Chinese laborers was employed to cut the trees and operate a paper mill (converted from an old ore-crushing mill) at Ravenna in nearby Soledad Canyon. So complete was the destruction of Joshua trees that a traveller through Palmdale in 1910 remarked on the complete absence of the trees in the vicinity of the train depot.

Apparently some of the wood was converted directly to pulp while the remainder was shredded and compressed into bales for shipment to London. The future of the Joshua tree looked bleak indeed. Joshua tree logs and shredded products were exhibited at agricultural fairs, and the manufacture of products from Joshua trees was hailed as a new industry. Rumors even circulated of converting all the paper mills on the west coast to produce the strong "cactus" paper for which raw material was "unlimited". Fortunately for the Joshua tree, the paper proved to be inferior and all the grandiose plans met with failure. But other men soon experimented with the soft wood of the desert tree.

Attempts were made to peel Joshua tree logs into thin, decorative veneers to be stained the colors of various woods. The huge amounts of dye absorbed by the porous Joshua tree wood quickly ended that scheme. More successful were the applications in which the soft, light Joshua tree wood was used as tree protectors, surgeon splints, artificial limbs, and break-away furniture for the film industry. For many years powdered Joshua tree wood was used to make beer foamier and to produce fluffier whipped cream and meringues.

Today's main economic interest in the Joshua tree, aside from its recognized scenic value to real estate brokers, is the production of steroids from its seed pods. One of these chemical agents has replaced the old sawdust additive in everything from beer to shaving creams. Other steroids are used in the medical field. Large parts of the Mojave Desert, as well as areas in Mexico where similar yuccas grow, are harvested annually for this valuable product.

The lonely tree of the Mojave has inspired many noble sentiments, but it has also played a role in the less honorable pursuits of man. One of the most outlandish examples is related by that iconoclastic chronicler of early-day Los Angeles, Major Horace Bell, in his *Reminiscences of a Ranger* (1927):

> The city [Los Angeles] began to increase its rate of growth about 1875, but it was still a slow movement until the boom struck in '85. This boom was one of the crimes of the age. Only a few people profited by it while hundreds of thousands were trapped into insane purchase of property and crazy speculation, and finally ruined. The daily press of Los Angeles boomed the boom from the word go. The writer of these lines was the only person having access to printer's ink that published a word of warning to the credulous. I was publishing a weekly paper then and did all that was possible to save people from ruin.
>
> I will give a few instances of the wildcatting during those memorable years. All the land from Redondo-by-the-Sea to Widneyville-by-the-Desert they cut up into town lots. They built cement sidewalks for miles into the desert fastness. They built railroad lines, where the main line did not run through, and took out train loads of crazy people with their pockets full of cash. Bands played gay music as they traveled. From

the trains they herded them into wagons, tallyhos or stages and hauled them to the heart of the proposed new "city." Here a vast array of refreshment tables would be set up in serried ranks, covered with cold lunch, while barrels of beer, whiskey and wine would be tapped to the blare of the band. All free of course, and most stimulating when the hour arrived for bidding in lots. Lots selling on those feast days for thousands of dollars apiece were afterward assessed for taxation at two dollars a lot and many of them reverted to the tax collector. My goodness, the colleges they proposed and sometimes actually built! A college for at least every thousand acres. The college seemed to be a big selling point. And hotels! Magnificent structures were actually erected that never held a guest after opening day and were later dedicated to the insurance companies by the fire route.

'Widneyville-by-the-Desert' was a prize exhibit of those days. The promoters referred to it as 'the modern Elysium,' I believe, or some such high-toned Greek brag. A tremendous excursion was organized to conduct the speculative hordes to the site of the proposed ideal city on the opening day. A natural and to the Eastern tenderfoot a rather appalling growth of cactus and yucca palms, commonly called Joshua trees, covered the desert hereabouts. These spiny, writhing Joshua trees are really a horrific sight if you are not used to them, but the promoters of Widneyville had a bright idea that saved them the expense of clearing the growth off. They did a little judicious trimming on the cactus plants and yuccas, shaping them up into a certain uniformity, then shipped out a carload of cheap wind-fall oranges and on the end of each bayonet-like spike on the yuccas and on each cactus spine they impaled an orange. Suddenly the desert fruited like the orange grove! Down the lines of the proposed streets staked out in the desert, and around the great square outlined by the surveyors, crowded innumerable orange trees loaded with their golden harvest. The Easterners stood agape at the Elysian sight, hardly listening to the salesmen as they described the college, the several churches, the great sanitarium and the magnificent hotel - temperance hotel - that would so soon surround the central plaza of Widneyville.

'Here, you see, ladies and gentlemen, is the natural home of the orange,' said the conductor of the excursion as he addressed the assembled multitude. 'These beautiful trees, so prolific of fruit, are a natural growth. This is the only spot west of the Rocky Mountains where the orange is indigenous. In a little while we will have irrigation canals all over the tract and when these orange trees are irrigated their fruit will grow as big as pumpkins. There'll be a fortune in every block, ladies and gentlemen.'

Blocks and blocks were sold from the plat of 'Widneyville-by-the-Desert,' at boom prices but no house was built on the actual site.

Oranges growing on Joshua trees is far-fetched, but the good folks of Nevada tried to do California one better. During the 1890s rumors floated across the sagebrush-covered basins into the Nevadan mining camps that banana trees had been successfully grafted onto Joshua trees. The desert would soon be covered by one gigantic banana plantation! William Manly's "brave little tree" has, like so many elements of our wilderness world, silently suffered and witnessed the foibles of mankind.

The population of Twenty-nine Palms at the time of my visit numbered two . . . one a prospector and old haunter of the locality, the other a consumptive from "inside" who was sacrificing every comfort of life for the sake of the dry air of this lonely spot, received me cordially enough, but remained convinced, I think , in spite of my plain story, that I was "lookin' up mineral, ain't you now?" They felt it an insult to their intelligence to be asked to believe that any one would come to Twenty-nine Palms in July for the sake of seeing the country and "them old pa'ms." "Country?" said the sick man, waving toward a sunset landscape that would have thrown Turner into a frenzy - "Country? Th' ain't no country round here to 'mount to nuthin'. You ever see any, Mac?" And Mac sententiously replied, "Durned if I ain't forgot what real country looks like, anyways."

J. Smeaton Chase

California Desert Trails, 1919

CHAPTER 5

THE OASIS OF MARA

FEATURES: Main Visitor Center, Park Headquarters, native fan palm oasis, ½-mile Oasis Nature Trail, botanical collection, bird life.

Anglo-American prospectors called it the Twentynine Palms Oasis, as it still appears on most maps, and from which the surrounding desert community derived its picturesque name. But to the Serrano Indians who inhabited the oasis in ages past, it was simply *Mara*, the 'place of small springs and much grass.' No other palm oasis of the California desert is more easily accessible, or possesses as long and colorful a history. Initially Indians, then gold-hunters and cattlemen, and finally health-seekers and desert lovers have received nurture beneath the graceful palms of Mara.

Water

Water no longer flows on the surface at Mara; the water table has dropped due to pumping of nearby wells. But water did flow here once, and in copious quantities, as attested to by the lingering name of "Indian Gardens" applied to the western end of the oasis where the native inhabitants maintained irrigated plots at the beginning of the twentieth century. Today's healthy palms, along with a profusion of mesquite and arrowweed, are reminders that water is still here, slowly seeping just beneath the surface.

But why should water magically appear at all on this desert plain? No canyon descends from a nearby snowcapped mountain range to funnel runoff toward Mara. Instead, the oasis owes its existence to the Pinto Mountain Fault. The land on one side of the fault has been displaced relative to the other side, resulting in the placement of a geologic formation less permeable to water on the north side of the

Oasis. Precipitation falling on the park highlands to the south rolls off the bare mountainsides, is absorbed into the sandy debris around their bases, and slowly percolates down the broad alluvial fan that spreads its apron toward the dry lake bed just north of Twentynine Palms. Part of this underground stream is intercepted and backed up behind the natural dam formed by the Pinto Mountain Fault, creating the Oasis of Mara. The east-west orientation of the fault is faithfully traced by the pattern of vegetation in the oasis. Utah Trail (the road out of Twentynine Palms on which the Visitor Center is located) leads up the huge alluvial fan to the true sources of Mara's water, the bare mountain slopes around Pinto Wye.

Oasis of Mara circa 1906

Indian Days

To the Indians the Oasis of Mara was much more than just a dependable water supply. Here was an abundance of useful plants to serve as direct food sources, as raw material for manufactured articles, and as ground cover to attract a plentiful supply of small game. Two of the most important plants were the native fan palm (*Washingtonia filifera*) and the honey mesquite (*Prosopis juliflora*). The hard, round seeds of the palm and the sugar-rich seed-pods of the mesquite were valuable food items. Both plants also supplied basic building materials - mesquite limbs providing the framework for palm frond structures that were both waterproof and windproof.

When Anglo-Americans first came to Mara during the latter part of the nineteenth century they found two tribes, the Serrano and the Chemehuevi, inhabiting the springs in peaceful coexistence. While the Serrano had ancestral claims to the oasis, the Chemehuevi were relative newcomers. The Serrano called this place *Mar-rah,* and they referred to themselves as the *Maringayam,* which white tongues corrupted into 'Morongo', a name now applied to a nearby Indian reservation as well as several local geographical features.

But by 1900 the majority of Indians at Mara were of the Chemehuevi tribe. These people represented a branch of the Southern Paiute stock that populated much of Nevada, Arizona and Utah. As the result of armed conflicts that broke out between the Chemehuevi and their fierce neighbors, the Mohaves, in 1867, the Chemehuevi had been displaced from their historic homelands along the Colorado River to Mara and other remote parts of the desert. When they arrived at

Mara, according to one source, they found it deserted, the Serrano having temporarily vacated the springs due to a smallpox epidemic. Over the years other Chemehuevi and Paiutes from as far away as southern Nevada, including the notorious Willie Boy, drifted into the oasis as the result of mounting white pressure on their traditional homelands. A 1902 census listed a total of 37 Indians at the Oasis of Mara, not exactly a teeming populace, but far outnumbering the permanent white residents.

There are many stories of the Indians at the oasis, constituting a large and interesting body of folklore in the history of Twentynine Palms. Certainly the most famous and well-documented incident revolved around the Willie Boy tragedy of 1909. Willie Boy, a Paiute Indian in his late twenties, was attracted by the charms of a young maiden named Isoleta, the daughter of Indian Mike Boniface, brother of 'Captain Jim' Boniface, the chief of the Chemehuevi residing at the Oasis of Mara. Meeting with disapproval from the father, Willie Boy decided to use whatever means necessary to obtain his heart's desire. He struck one night when Indian Mike and his family were encamped at the Gilman Ranch northwest of Banning, slaying Indian Mike and escaping with Isoleta in tow. A posse formed and trailed Willie Boy and his captive up through Morongo Valley to a region called The Pipes, where they discovered the body of Isoleta shot through the back. Evidently the girl had proven too much of a burden.

Days passed with the posse occasionally just missing the crafty Paiute. Willie Boy eventually made his way to the Indian village at the Oasis of Mara where he had planned to recover a cache of ammunition. But news of his depredations had preceded him. Instead, he found only one old squaw who had thrown the precious cartridges into a pool to thwart him from committing additional murders. The chase continued several more days before he was cornered in the foothills of the San Bernardino Mountains. There, after a gunfight in which one member of the posse was wounded, Willie Boy ended his life rather than undergo the disgrace of capture and trial.

A thorough and fascinating account of Willie Boy is related by Harry Lawton in his book *Willie Boy, A Desert Manhunt* (Paisano Press, 1960), from which the popular movie *Tell Them Willie Boy Was Here* was adapted.

Within a few years of the Willie Boy episode the Indians completely vacated Mara. Today the only visible reminder of their former presence is the one-acre Indian Cemetery located on Adobe Road near the west end of the oasis, the site of the Indian Gardens of yesteryear. Unmarked graves bear silent witness to the first people to find shelter beneath the palms of Mara.

Explorers

In all likelihood the first Anglo-American to visit the Oasis of Mara was Pauline Weaver, the legendary mountain man, gold-hunter, and army scout. In 1842, when California was still part of Mexico, Weaver was in residence at San Gorgonio Pass near the present site of Banning, California. His Chemehuevi Indian wife and their son were living with the tribe along the Colorado River below Needles, California. Perhaps guided by Indian friends, Weaver, in order to visit his distant family, pioneered a route to the Colorado River that passed up through Morongo Valley, turned east to the Oasis of Mara, and continued from there on across the desert. "Weaver's Road" remained a little-used route for many years, known only to the few who dared to travel into the stark landscape of the southern Mojave Desert.

The first recorded mention of the Oasis of Mara is in a report of Colonel Henry Washington's San Bernardino Base Line Survey in 1855. The survey map shows an "Old Road to the Providence Mountains" leading east from the Oasis, in all probability the old Weaver Road. A year later A.P. Green, working in conjunction with Colonel Washington, passed through the same neighborhood and mentioned the "trail to Palm Springs", noting that there were "26 fine large palm trees in Section 33 from which the springs take their name 'Palm Springs'." The name "Palm Springs" was retained until the 1870s when the name 'Twentynine Palms' came into common usage. Whether or not there were ever exactly 29 palm trees growing at the Oasis will probably never be known.

Two Colorful Pioneers

By the 1860s the great gold rush to the Sierra Nevada's Mother Lode Country had subsided and the argonauts began fanning out across the remote regions of California, even into the dreaded deserts. The Oasis of Mara naturally came to serve as a jumping-off point into the desert. Prospectors camped beside its quiet pools of life-sustaining water, exchanging news of claims and prospects. In 1865 the Jeff Davis Mine was located in Rattlesnake Canyon a few miles west of Twentynine Palms, becoming the first deposit to be filed on in what was soon known as the Palms District. The first Anglo-Americans to assume permanent residence at the Oasis were prospectors attracted to the new desert diggings - Bill McHaney and John "Quartz" "Chuckawalla" "Dirtyshirt" "Charley" Wilson.

Bill McHaney, who settled at the oasis in 1879, may have had his first introduction to the area while he and his brother Jim were engaged in cattle operations around the Big Bear Lake area in the nearby San Bernardino Mountains. Like the cattlemen of a later generation, the McHaneys may have used the high meadows around Big Bear for summer range and driven their cattle down to the Twentynine Palms region for winter grazing. Evidently Bill McHaney divided his time between the Oasis of Mara and the brothers' emerging cattle operation located up in the Queen Mountains southwest of Twentynine Palms. According to Bill Keys, who came into ownership of the Desert Queen Ranch, both McHaneys came to what became the Desert Queen Ranch in 1879 and started a profitable and highly suspect cattle "business". (More regarding this phase of activity is contained in the chapters dealing with Hidden Valley, the Desert Queen Ranch and the Desert Queen Mine.)

For at least a 16-year period Bill McHaney did maintain a modest cabin at Mara, as well as a primitive shelter made of flattened 5-gallon tin cans in nearby Music Valley. Widely known and liked throughout the district, he claimed to have established such good relations with the native inhabitants of the Oasis that they revealed to him the trails, waterholes, and even some gold sources in the surrounding desert. That he became an expert on the geography of the district was proven in his later years by the invaluable assistance he provided Elizabeth C. Campbell in completing her archeological reconnaissance of the Twentynine Palms region for the Southwest Museum.

Beloved old Bill McHaney passed away in 1937, spending his last days under the care of the Keys family at the Desert Queen Ranch. He perpetrated one last prank on his friends in Twentynine Palms by being a day late for his own funeral due to snow storms blocking the roads from the Desert Queen Ranch.

Wild antelope still roamed the Twentynine Palms region when Bill McHaney arrived in 1879. Here the old-timer poses, rifle at rest, in front of his primitive cabin made from flattened 5-gallon tins. (photo courtesy JTNP)

Quartz" Wilson was a true eccentric. He arrived at Mara in 1883 and stayed for many years until the county removed him in his dotage. In the shade of the palms he built himself a dugout cabin and an arrastra (a primitive ore crushing device).

Wilson developed a reputation for boasting about his "fabulous" mines. When he would find a party gullible enough to bankroll an investigative trip, Wilson would first take them out on the surrounding desert for one or two days to show them the "lay of the land". Another day or two would be spent scratching up interesting "color" at some possible prospects. Finally Wilson would confess to his by now totally exasperated backers that his mine was nothing more than a poor prospect hole.

Despite these shenanigans, Wilson was not a bad prospector. In the 1880s he and Tom Lyons filed the discovery claim on the Virginia Dale east of Twentynine Palms, setting off a minor stampede into what eventually developed into the extensive Dale Mining District. A few years later, while taking a shortcut to Indio, Wilson stumbled across a gold-laced boulder that assayed out at 500 dollars. The location became the Eldorado Mine, the extensive workings of which may still be viewed by taking a rugged hike in the foothills bordering the western edge of Pinto Basin. Like many a single-blanket prospector, for Wilson the searching and finding of gold was more important than the subsequent development of a paying mine. Wilson always sold off his interests before the payoff developed, electing instead to pursue the free life of the prospector. Near the Eldorado is Wilson Wash, through which a portion of the park highway passes on its way to Pinto Basin, preserving in its name the spirit of the old prospector who once probed its steep canyon walls for hidden bonanzas.

Death Visits the Oasis

Mines sprang up all around the little Oasis of Mara, and mines are more than just holes in the ground. The machinery, food supplies and timber required by these ventures could not be generated locally. These necessities were hauled in from such distant places as San Bernardino, Amboy and Indio. Mara, with its never-failing supply of water and grass, became a focus of freighting activity, and heavy wagons pulled by long teams of horses and mules became commonplace at the oasis. Most of the present roads in the park follow the old teamster routes. The men who operated the big rigs worked long hours in an often hostile environment, so the cool shade of the oasis was a precious commodity to them.

Death rode beside one teamster and his passengers on a wagon bound for the mines of Dale. A Mrs. Whallon, who had accepted a job as a cook at the mines, had hoped that the desert would present a cure to her ailing 18 year-old daughter. Instead, the long, arduous journey from Banning on a slow-moving, bone-jarring freight wagon had taken its final toll. Even the haven of Mara could not stave off the inevitable. There on March 10, 1905, Maria Eleanor Whallon was laid to rest in a lonely grave beneath the palms. No other women were at the oasis to provide comfort to the girl's mother, but Mrs. Whallon is reported to have remarked on the extreme kindness of the teamster Pete Domac. The Oasis Nature Trail passes within a few feet of where the young woman reposes, still sheltered by two guardian palms and marked by a simple headstone of Pinto gneiss.

There are other reminders of the days of the wagoners at the oasis. The cottonwoods, willows and one old fig tree growing among the palms and mesquite were planted by the freight haulers, the willows supposedly sprouting from willow whips plucked by the teamsters while passing through Big Morongo Canyon on their long haul from San Bernardino and Banning. Their corrals and support structures have since crumbled to dust, but the teamsters' living legacy remains.

Cattlemen

The grass and water of Mara attracted cattlemen as well as prospectors and teamsters. By the 1870s the surrounding region was already being exploited as winter range. The most active of all the cattle outfits in the first three decades of the twentieth century was the partnership of C.O. Barker and William Shay. Barker Dam (Chapter 10) dates from the period when Barker and Shay stock roamed throughout most of the high valleys in the western part of the park. The cattlemen constructed other small reservoirs, or "tanks", that can be visited in the park: White Tank, Squaw Tank, Live Oak Tank, Ivanpah Tank, Grand Tank, and others less prominent. They also dug wells, including the one located just off the Oasis Nature Trail excavated by Barker and Shay cowboys around 1900.

Health-seekers Establish a Town

The pleasant community of Twentynine Palms owes its existence first to the water of Mara and second to Dr. James Luckie of Pasadena, California, who sent disabled World War I veterans to the Twentynine Palms region in the hopes that the climate would alleviate or cure their chronic ailments. Not too surprisingly, many invalids when exposed to the dry air and bright sun of the desert along with a more active mode of living were completely cured after a short stay at Mara. Some health-seekers elected to remain in the area, representing the first stable element around which the town of Twentynine Palms eventually formed.

For many of these early settlers the Oasis provided them with their first desert home. A whole family might encamp beneath the palms until they could prove up on a homestead and erect a house. Many a pioneer resident of Twentynine Palms cooked meals over a mesquite fire at the Oasis.

Paradise Threatened

As has happened too often in our beautiful country, each little Shangri-La attracts greater and greater numbers of people until these small pieces of paradise-on-Earth have in many cases been literally loved to death. It may be happening here as well. Mara, whose refreshing waters nurtured the beginnings of Twentynine Palms, is now threatened by a man-made drought caused by the continued growth of the human community surrounding it. The last recorded flow of surface water at Mara was in 1942, just before the establishment of the Twentynine Palms Marine Base with its concomitant increase in population, a population making greater demands on a limited supply of underground water. Today one has to go down ten feet or more before encountering the water table at Mara. Continued pumping of nearby wells will result in additional lowering of the water table. Will the old palms shrivel and die? How will young trees sprout on the dry surface? The little Oasis of Mara reflects a situation common throughout the rest of the Southwest, where overdraft of underground aquifers to serve ever-growing populations has become a universal problem.

Important Plants - the Fan Palm and Mesquite

Endemic to the Colorado Desert, the native fan palm (*Washingtonia filifera*) approaches its northernmost distribution in the five palm oases of Joshua Tree National Park. The palms that decorate so many streets of Southern California and Arizona are the descendants of these native trees of the Colorado Desert, now outnumbering their cousins in the wild. To the Indians this "Prince of Vegetables", as one author described it, was far more than an attractive ornamental. The seeds, unlike the luscious fruit of the date palm, consist of small, hard, round pits covered by a thin layer of sweet flesh. They grow in great abundance and were relished by the native peoples. The palm fronds were valued as a building material; a carefully thatched house was both waterproof and windproof.

For Indians such as the Agua Caliente branch of the Cahuilla tribe, who dwelled in proximity to the great palm canyons adjacent to Palm Springs, California, the native palm assumed an important role in tribal mythology. One of their legends explains the origin of the palm as the desire of an old man to benefit his people. He transformed himself into the first palm tree, whereupon the people soon discovered the sweet fruit and carried the seeds to all the places where palm trees now grow on the desert.

The most prominent understory plant at the Oasis of Mara and one of the most important plants in the lives of the native peoples of the Southwest is the honey mesquite (*Prosopis juliflora*). Certainly few plants of this hemisphere can claim a more noble heritage. For according to Mexican legend, the great god Quetzalcoatl, in displeasure at the Aztec priesthood's persistence in maintaining the horrid feature of human sacrifice, transformed all the cacao trees of Mexico into *mizquitl*, that is mesquite, before departing over the sea never to return. However, Quetzalcoatl's curse evidently was more far-reaching than Mexico, for mesquite thickets are to be found all the way from the southwestern United States down through Central and South America into the Argentine.

The mesquite appears to have been far more of a blessing to the native population than a curse. In a land not noted for its fruitfulness, the mesquite provided a reliable source of nutritious beans which were gathered and stored in large, woven granary baskets (supported off the ground, more often than not, by mesquite-wood posts). The beans were typically ground into a coarse flour (usually in a mortar made from a thick mesquite limb) which could be reconstituted later in the form of thick mush cakes.

Mesquite wood was used for a variety of purposes: the manufacture of fire-hardened arrow foreshafts, for house frames, and, of course, as firewood. The bark provided wrapping material and, when pounded, could be woven into skirts and carrying nets. The gum exuded by the plant was used as an all-purpose adhesive, or it could be diluted to use on wounds or as an eye wash. But of all the uses the native Americans developed for the mesquite, one above all others can still be equally appreciated by modern man - shade - the coolest on the desert due to the way the plant's leaflets are hinged to allow passage of the slightest breeze.

Mesquite thickets have often served as an indicator of sub-surface water, and many a desert pioneer has sunk a successful well where heavy mesquite growth occurred. But the plant can be deceptive, sometimes going to incredible extremes in its search for water. Biologist Raymond Cowles recorded having traced an exposed mesquite root horizontally for 180 feet before it suddenly turned downward. From the reduction in root size in the first 180 feet, he estimated that the root may have penetrated downward for another 100 feet or so. The unruffled Cowles admitted that his was a goodly length for a root, "but in its way it matches other accomplishments of this remarkable tree."

A Gathering of Vultures

Twice each year, around Easter and in October, a great flock of turkey vultures converges on Mara. For a few days only, hundreds of dark silhouettes may be seen gracefully gliding overhead or roosting in the palms and cottonwoods. For millennia these scavengers have been conducting their rendezvous, assembling in the fall to migrate to points south, then returning in the spring to disperse from this common site to their far-flung summer homes. The phenomenon is duplicated at numerous points along the Colorado River. Curiously, not all the vultures of the desert partake in the annual migration; many remain behind, content as year-round residents.

Even when vultures are not gathered at the Oasis, it is a bird watcher's delight, where quiet hours spent wandering with binoculars will be richly rewarding. A favorite feathered inhabitant sure to be observed by anyone who carefully looks for it, is the phainopepla. Black as coal except for white wing patches flashed in flight, it resembles in shape the eastern cardinal, complete with headcrest. The phainopepla consumes the berries of the mistletoe that infest the mesquite of the oasis. The mucilaginous seeds pass through the bird's digestive tract and are discharged unharmed, often upon fresh mesquite limbs, thus spreading the mistletoe and increasing the size of the phainopepla's berry garden.

...it is not all external, what the oasis gives. The heart beats easier, the pulses are less strong and masterful, the nerves are more under control, and the inward fever of body and brain seems quenched almost as soon as one reclines under the shade of the oasis. And then, penetrating farther, mind and soul are soothed and quieted, and one is able to see how to use the added strength and rugged power he has absorbed from the rude and uncouth, but loving and generous bosom of the desert mother.

George Wharton James

Wonders of the Colorado Desert, 1906

CHAPTER 6

FORTYNINE PALMS OASIS

FEATURES: Native fan palm oasis, bighorn sheep area, 3-mile round-trip hike on maintained trail.

The mile-and-a-half trail to Fortynine Palms Oasis follows an old Indian pathway up and over a ridge populated by colorful barrel cacti. The trail may be closed at certain times of the year due to fire hazard. The hike is more strenuous than any of the nature trails in the park, involving a 400-foot climb going into the Oasis and a 300-foot ascent on the return, but the grove of stately palms shading a quiet pool of water surrounded by the wild and rocky canyon more than compensates for the effort. Occasionally, desert bighorn sheep are sighted drinking at the pool or scrambling up the cliffsides. The trail to Fortynine Palms Oasis is exposed to sun, and hikers should carry extra amounts of water (the water at the oasis is not potable). Picnickers should carry out all their trash. An entertaining game for energetic children is to provide them with plastic garbage bags so they can assist in picking up any litter at the oasis or on the trail.

Almost all the palm trees at this site are missing their long skirts of dead fronds, exposing blackened trunks from the fires that periodically sweep the canyon. Despite the apparent severity of the burns, the palms have survived the holocausts healthier than ever. Perhaps fires actually aid the palms by consuming the dense understory of mesquite, a serious water competitor, or by destroying insect pests living in the crowns of the trees. It is known that the Indians living in the canyons near Palm Springs occasionally fired the palms to increase their fruitfulness, so evidently fire plays an important role in palm tree ecology.

Of the five palm oases in Joshua Tree, Fortynine Palms is the only one hosting the California palm-borer (*Dinapate wrightii*), a beetle that can cause extensive damage to a living tree. An infestation begins when the Dinapate eggs are laid in the tender leaf bud atop the towering trunk. The hatched larvae devour their way deep into the pithy core of the plant. Entomologist H.G. Hubbard described the results of such activities: "It is hard to realize the enormous extent of the Dinapate galleries. If one finds 20 to 30 holes in one of the Washingtonia palms, the interior probably is entirely eaten out from end to end, and one can follow the frass-filled galleries, over one inch in diameter, for 20 feet up and down the trunk following the grain and without diminishing sensibly in size. Then think of the yards and yards of smaller galleries made by the larvae while still young. Such extensive and prodigious borings cannot be made in one or two years, and certainly not in any trunk of moderate size for it would not yield enough food."

The feeding grubs can be heard as they eat, their powerful mandibles making quite audible clicking sounds. An experiment worth performing is to put an ear to a tree in the Fortynine Palms Oasis and listen for a sound similar to fingernails clicking together, indicating the home of the rare Dinapate beetle.

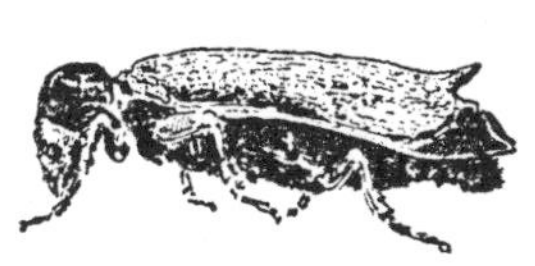

Dinapate wrightii

. . . . for after each day was done and our wolfish hunger appeased with a hot supper of fried bacon, bread, molasses and black coffee, the pipe-smoking, song-singing and yarn-spinning around the evening camp-fire in the still solitudes of the desert was a happy, care-free sort of recreation that seemed the very summit and culmination of earthly luxury. It is a kind of life that has a potent charm for all men, whether city or country-bred. . . We all confess to a gratified thrill at the thought of "camping out."

Mark Twain
Roughing It, 1872

CHAPTER 7

INDIAN COVE AND RATTLESNAKE CANYON

FEATURES: Rock formations, nature trail, seasonal stream.

Indian Cove

The boulderland surrounding Indian Cove Campground is a delight to explore. Huge, fanciful outcrops of quartz monzonite provide a natural playground for children and adults. Campers are often entertained by the astounding gymnastics of rockclimbers responding to the challenge of "Billboard Buttress", "Campfire Crag", "Moosedog Tower", "Feudal Wall", and a dozen other popular climbs.

The area around the campground is botanically rich, and with reference books in hand one can tackle the flat terrain around the bases of the boulder-piles with as much enthusiasm as the rockclimbers their heights. A quarter-mile nature trail at the far western end of the campground road provides an excellent introduction to the native flora.

Indian Cove is possibly the oldest campground in the park; in ancient times it was a popular stopping place for the Indians. Ollas (pottery vessels used to store a supply of food) are still occasionally discovered in and around the campground, hidden in rock crevices where these earliest transients cached them for future consumption. (Note: Finds of this nature should always be left undisturbed and immediately reported to the park rangers.)

Moonshiners also found Indian Cove to their liking. Hidden up in the rocks south of the road turnaround where the nature trail begins is Sneakeye Spring, where lame John Stull maintained a still during Prohibition days. The Twentynine Palms region, reached only by long, rough dirt roads, was sufficiently removed from the long arm of the law to become a center for the manufacture of white lightnin'. Stull's still must have been a regular stop on the old "Sullivan Road", the forerunner of today's Highway 62, which explains why the road came to be known as the "Bootlegger's Highway."

Rattlesnake Canyon

No weekend camping trip to Indian Cove would be complete without a scramble up Rattlesnake Canyon. The rocky defile, often reverberating to the sounds of rushing water, is only a short walk east from the picnic area at the eastern end of the campground road. The wide, sandy wash, when followed upstream, soon becomes choked with huge boulders, a few of which are studded with large pink feldspar crystals. The appearance of large crystals in rocks such as these indicates a longer cooling period from the molten state and a slightly different chemical composition from the main mass of molten material from which the rock was formed due to contact with existing rock of a different composition. This type of contact zone is present in Rattlesnake Canyon where the eastern side of the canyon is composed of dark-colored Pinto gneiss while the west side consists of light-pink quartz monzonite. (Another striking example of feld-sparthic crystallization can be more easily observed in the boulders delimiting the parking areas in the Indian Cove Group Camp.) A desert rarity, a stream of running water, is sometimes encountered a short distance into the boulder field at the entrance to Rattlesnake Canyon, especially in early spring. Farther upstream, steep, water-polished cliffs bar the way, although good climbers can surmount them. Potholes filled with excess runoff, separated by delicate waterfalls in season, play host to myriad numbers of diminutive *Hylas*, the tree frogs whose high-pitched peepings echo through the canyon during their nightly serenades.

Somewhere in Rattlesnake Canyon is the long-abandoned site of the earliest recorded mine of the Twentynine Palms region, the Jeff Davis (1865), and perhaps the remains of a Mexican-type smelter of a much earlier era.

The desert asks not just your heart but your mind and a bit of your time, since to appreciate the harmonies of so hostile a land you must understand relationships that do not reveal themselves readily. The huge scale of the desert is easily grasped, even by looking only through car windows at seventy miles per hour; but the intricacies and the small miracles withhold themselves - the tiny cascade of sand grains as a lizard bolts for safety, the royal purple spots at the base of each petal of a mallow blossom, the eyes of a kit fox or a kangaroo rat reflecting the glow of your campfire.

Ruth Kirk

Desert, *The American Southwest*, 1973

CHAPTER 8

COVINGTON FLATS, EUREKA PEAK, BLACK ROCK CANYON CAMPGROUND

FEATURES: Giant Joshua trees, Eureka Peak viewpoint, Black Rock Canyon Campground, Hi-View and South Park Peak trails.

Covington Flats

The dirt road leading into the Covington Flats country is narrow in places and should not be attempted by automobiles towing trailers. If the weather has been wet recently, it would be advisable to inquire at the Black Rock Campground or at park headquarters in Twentynine Palms about road conditions before tackling this trip. Usually the road is in good shape, and careful driving should get all but the lowest of low-slung vehicles to the destinations described herein.

Old Will Covington, for whom the flats were named, was a pioneer Morongo Valley rancher. In the early decades of the twentieth century he was instrumental in erecting life-saving road signs throughout much of the surrounding desert. Apparently he once established a mining claim in Lower Covington Flat, possibly as a means to secure rights to a water supply for his cattle operation. Today the only sign of man's impact in Lower Covington Flat is the dirt access road and the picnic tables located in the small grove of Joshua trees at the end of the road.

Upper Covington Flat is one of the author's favorite picnic locations. The road terminates at the edge of a forest of giant Joshua trees. The largest specimen in the park, approximately 36 feet high and 14 feet in circumference, stands about 30 yards south of the road turnaround. Other giants nearly as large as the champion are scattered over the landscape. An hour or a day can be spent in exploration and communion with the grizzled patriarchs of Upper Covington Flat.

The giant Joshua trees of Upper Covington Flat dwarf human explorers

Eureka Peak

The view from the 5,516-foot summit of Eureka Peak is one of the finest in the park. The 10,000-foot upthrust of Mt. San Jacinto behind Palm Springs is visible off to the southwest, while nearer at hand, directly west, looms the rounded hulk of the San Gorgonio massif, a cluster of 10,000-foot peaks crowned by San Gorgonio Mountain itself, at 11,499 feet the highest point in Southern California. This is a view to take in during the spring when the high peaks are covered with glistening snow. Access to the peak is by means of the same road that traverses both Lower and Upper Covington Flats. The road turnaround ends about a hundred yards southeast of the summit, which can be reached by an easy footpath. In winter, snow often lies on the ground in this high corner of the park.

Black Rock Canyon Campground

Black Rock Canyon Campground, with its easy access to the restaurants in Yucca Valley, is an ideal destination for the family wishing to go camping without saddling someone with the chores of cooking and dishwashing. Its 4,000-foot elevation makes it one of the coolest, and in mid-winter, coldest, campgrounds in Joshua Tree. Campsites are located amid a forest of Joshua trees. A large building houses an auditorium and ranger station, and provides some shelter for winter campers when the cold winds blow. In spring and fall, the area is a delight; even in summer fairly moderate temperatures prevail.

Hiking trails emanate in all directions from the campground. A map showing routes and destinations is usually posted at the ranger station. This high country sports a growth of pinyons and junipers offering habitat for mule deer and the elusive bighorn sheep, so hikers should keep alert for wildlife.

Hi-view and South Park Peak Trails

Reached via a short dirt road leading west from the campground entrance, the 1.3-mile Hi-View Nature Trail and the 5/8-mile South Park Peak Trail provide introductions to desert flora as well as an excellent view of Yucca Valley.

The abrupt 10,000-foot wall of Mt. San Jacinto looms over the upper Coachella Valley in this view from Eureka Peak

Under high cliffs and far from the huge town I sit me down.

Coventry Patmore

CHAPTER 9

HIDDEN VALLEY

FEATURES: Hidden Valley Campground, Hidden Valley Trail, rock formations, rockclimbing activities.

Hidden Valley resembles a surrealistic moonscape; monolithic quartz monzonite buttes and towers thrust out of the earth like worn dragon's teeth. This weird scenery was familiar to generations of Indians, as the many pictographs (rock paintings), petroglyphs (symbols carved into rocks), and deeply worn bedrock mortars attest.

Legends

The colorful stories of Hidden Valley begin with the arrival of the white man. Legend has it that the rock-rimmed valley, situated in a remote and then largely unexplored desert, served as the headquarters for a large-scale cattle and horse rustling operation. What has been fairly well established is that two brothers, Jim and Bill McHaney, arrived in the Hidden Valley area in 1879. The rest of the story is a blend of folklore and fact, repeated so often by now as to make the separation of the two nearly impossible.

It appears that the McHaney brothers were pressed from two different molds. While Bill was basically an honest and likable fellow, brother Jim possessed a streak of wildness that attracted men of like nature into the McHaney cattle operation. Among those with ties to the "McHaney Gang" were Ike Chestnut, George Myers, Charley Martin (who had served sixteen years in prison for shooting two men in San Jacinto and was later involved in a killing over the Desert Queen Mine), Willie Button (whom legend credits with the discovery of the narrow entrance to Hidden Valley), and Charley Button (both Button brothers eventually met their fates in a barroom brawl).

The McHaney operation consisted of "obtaining" horses in Arizona to exchange for cattle in California. The procedure might be reversed depending on the relative "availability" of stock at either end of the trail. Regardless of final destination, the stolen animals were rebranded and fattened on the grasses in and around Hidden Valley.

The events of a clandestine activity on the remote California desert a hundred years ago were not recorded in detail, so that today even the exact location of the original Hidden Valley is a matter of conjecture. The late Bill Keys, pioneer rancher who came to the area in 1910 and befriended Bill McHaney, insisted that the real Hidden Valley was the canyon now inundated behind a crude dam built by Keys behind the Desert Queen Ranch. But the present Hidden Valley might just as easily have served the disreputable aims of the McHaney Gang.

Hidden Valley Today

Now only two-footed human critters hoof it through the narrow entrance and around the 1.4-mile loop trail enclosed by the rocky walls of Hidden Valley. Inside the cliff-girt sanctuary, the visitor is greeted by a stony menagerie of animals, human faces, architectural and abstract forms frozen in the quartz monzonite turrets and walls surrounding the valley. There is no mistaking the Trojan staring down from his post in the rocks on the right as you enter the valley and approach the fork in the trail. A word of caution - the northern half of the loop trail requires a modest ability at boulder-scrambling.

The Trojan

Hidden Valley Campground

The geological wonders of Joshua Tree National Park attract rockclimbers from all over Southern California, and the focal point of their activities is at the intersection of the Hidden Valley Campground road and the park highway. The campground, surrounded by dramatic rock towers nicknamed "The Blob", "Cyclops", "Pee Wee", and "Rock Hudson", is always crowded with men and women in rough clothing carrying ropes and other strange paraphernalia peculiar to the sport of rockclimbing. Perhaps these activities are what make Hidden Valley Campground the most popular in the park. Even if all the camping spaces are filled, it is worth a visit just to take advantage of the free entertainment.

Rockclimbers from all over Southern California congregate on the outcrops surrounding the Hidden Valley area. These activities should be attempted only by trained mountaineers.

It is one wild chaotic upheaval and tumblement of disintegrating coarse granite. Great masses, of irregular size and shape, thrust their heads above the general mass, and stand, split, seamed, creviced, shattered, jagged, and rough and in some cases rounded by water and weather, in dumb protest against the fierceness of the desert sun.

George Wharton James
Wonders of the Colorado Desert, 1906

CHAPTER 10

BARKER DAM AND THE WONDERLAND OF ROCKS

FEATURES: Barker Dam Loop Trail, bird life, rock formations, petroglyphs and bedrock mortars.

Northeast of Hidden Valley Campground is a masterpiece of geology known as the Wonderland of Rocks; a confusing, jumbled, elaborately jointed and eroded mass of quartz monzonite sprawls over several thousand acres. The complex heart of this rock wilderness is not traversed by any trail and even experienced hikers must use the utmost care to prevent disorientation on cross-country rambles.

Barker Dam

The safest and easiest way to sample the Wonderland of Rocks is to hike the 1.1-mile Barker Dam Loop Trail. A bladed dirt road leads from the Hidden Valley Campground to the Barker Dam parking area. Concrete slabs on the southwest side of the parking area are reminders of the 1950s when this was private property. The slabs mark the site where wild animals were kept by a film crew working on a popular nature movie. Occupying a spot farther out in the flat was Bill McHaney's cabin, where the old-timer spent his last days under the care of the Keys family.

The trail to Barker Dam begins at the north end of the parking area. In a few steps the visitor is transported into a rocky alcove typical of hundreds of others in the Wonderland of Rocks. Turbinella oaks (*Quercus turbinella*) shade the hiker while the high-pitched, bird-like calls of Beechey ground squirrels (*Citellus beecheyi*) may be heard scolding intruders. From here the trail enters a narrow passage leading northward between rock walls to emerge upon a body of water (provided enough rain has fallen). A short scramble around the left shoreline delivers one at the dam site. Many species of birds not normally associated with desert habitat are drawn to the pond.

A considerable body of water is retained behind Barker Dam in occasional wet years.

There was probably a natural catchment in this stone-girt canyon when the McHaneys operated their cattle "business" during the 1880s. Later, cowboys under the direction of George Myers constructed a small dam upstream of the present large structure. At times of low water this old dam may still be seen. Still later, C.O. Barker constructed the base of the present dam, which was finally raised to its present height during the 1950s by the Keys family. Bill Keys re-titled the structure "Bighorn Dam" and an inscription bearing that name along with the names of the Keys family members is located on top of the south buttress of the dam.

The face of Barker Dam clearly shows the improvements made by its several owners.

The trail virtually disappears at the dam site but can be picked up again by scrambling down the boulders on the south (near) side of the dam. At the dam's base is one of Bill Keys' unique watering troughs. A float control mechanism similar to that found in most flush toilets was contained in the center of the circular trough, protected from curious cattle by an inner stone wall.

From the base of the dam the trail curves back southward, traversing a flat populated by Joshua trees and surrounded by picturesque rock formations. A huge boulder known as Piano Rock squats in the middle of the flat, its name a holdover from when the area was under private ownership and a piano was installed on its summit for the entertainment of equestrian groups. The numerous recumbent Joshua tree trunks were used both as benches for the riders and hitching rails for their mounts.

Beyond Piano Rock is a trail junction. The right hand fork leads to the "movie petroglyphs" a hundred feet beyond the junction. This is another reminder of the period when the area was under private ownership. Apparently there are genuine petroglyphs at this site, which were painted to provide contrast required to make them more easily photographed for a movie. The film crew probably added a few creations of their own. (Please note: This was a deplorable act of individuals ignorant of the rarity of these mysterious renderings by the aboriginal Indians. Anyone caught defacing rocks in the park, especially if destruction of pictographs or petroglyphs is involved, is liable to prosecution under the law.)

After inspecting the "movie petroglyphs", the visitor should return to the trail junction and take the other fork. In the first dozen yards several bedrock mortars can be found by paralleling the trail along the base of the cliffs to the right, after which the trail can be regained and followed the last few hundred feet to where it completes its circuit in the little alcove first entered from the parking area.

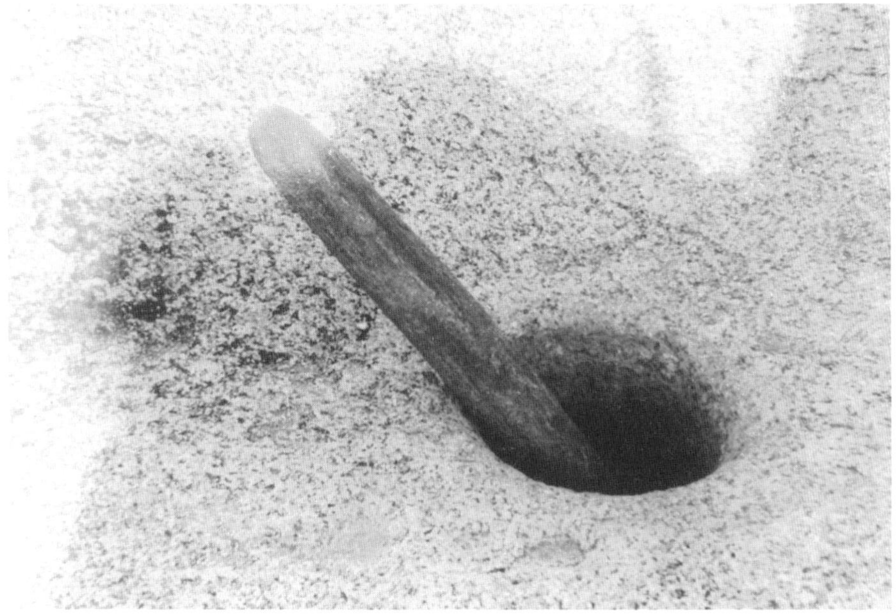

Bedrock mortars scattered throughout the Wonderland of Rocks attest to the wealth of edible seeds available to early aboriginal inhabitants.

. . . if you spend any time on the western deserts, you will find not a few of their sparsely scattered inhabitants are there because they are non-conformists. The drums which keep the majority marching along in the cities make no appeal to them. They hear another music. That some people should prefer living on nothing in the wilderness to living in town with television and all the trimmings is a fact which is good for the rest of us to know, and occasionally to think about. . . Every man should be allowed to keep step to the music he hears.

Aldous Huxley

CHAPTER 11

THE DESERT QUEEN RANCH

FEATURES: Regularly conducted tours of a former working ranch preserved to show man's adaptation to a desert environment.

The Desert Queen Ranch lies tucked away in a rock-bound amphitheater in the western edge of the Wonderland of Rocks. Access is by a dirt road out of the Hidden Valley Campground.

The ranch has been carefully preserved in its working state as an example of how man adapted to the arid environment of the desert. Farming and mining equipment as well as the day-to-day utensils of domestic life lie about as if their owners had walked away yesterday. The Desert Queen Ranch teaches more than just how people coped with living on the desert; it is a graphic example of an independent way of life formerly shared by most Americans but now rapidly disappearing, if not already extinct, under the onslaught of a modern technological society.

Due to the ease with which artifacts can be picked up and carried away by vandals, the Desert Queen Ranch is opened only to small, escorted groups. Any other type of entry without the express permission of the National Park Service is prohibited. Regular tours are conducted almost every weekend on a first-come basis. Tour schedules are posted at the visitor centers and in the campgrounds.

The modern history of the Desert Queen Ranch is inseparable from that of William F. Keys. For over fifty years of his life, until his death in 1969, Bill Keys expended his considerable energy on the ranch and the surrounding desert. He brought a bride here and with her raised a family; he grew his crops and grazed his cattle; he built dams to retain the slightest rain runoff and laid pipes to irrigate gardens and water stock; he worked his mines and scavenged every abandoned claim within reach for anything that might be of conceivable use around the ranch; he built the road out to Keys View to work his Hidden Gold Mine. At the ranch Keys constructed the little machine shop and forge, the corrals and fences, the stone walls, and even a school house for his offspring and the children of neighboring homesteaders. Bill Keys worked hard to win his home from the desert and he fought hard to protect it; he went to prison for that. But the story of the Desert Queen Ranch properly begins long before Bill Keys ever set foot on it.

The main ranch house of the Desert Queen Ranch, along with many outbuildings and equipment, appears as though its former owners had walked away from it yesterday.

Early Inhabitants

A steady trickle of water along the bottom of an isolated canyon in the heart of the desert made it possible for plants to flourish, in turn sheltering and nourishing hoards of small game. A wandering band of Indians discovered and exploited this oasis of life. Pictographs and petroglyphs, the rock art of these ancient ones, abound in the hills surrounding the Desert Queen Ranch. Further evidence of their occupancy is visible where the road cuts through a low berm near the entrance to the ranch proper. A dark strata in the exposed cut marks the location of an Indian midden, or refuse heap, where generation after generation gathered around a communal campfire. On the opposite side of the adjacent streambed a little farther upstream are bedrock mortars used by the Indian women to reduce hard seeds to a coarse flour. That is about all that is known of these earliest inhabitants. Only the canyon walls know when they arrived and when they departed.

The first structure encountered on a tour of the ranch is a crumbling adobe barn. It was erected about 1893 by the first white men to use the canyon, the McHaney brothers. It is conjectured that the McHaneys initially came into the area in 1879 in search of a secluded location to engage in their cattle operation. (The story of the McHaney Gang's use of Hidden Valley for their cattle rustling activities is related in Chapter 9.)

The McHaneys eventually transferred their interest to mining by developing the nearby Desert Queen Mine (Chapter 16). Jim McHaney soon squandered the profits, lost control of the mine, and drifted to parts unknown (legend purports that he ended up in prison on a counterfeiting conviction).

The McHaneys had established an ore-crushing mill in their canyon stronghold, so when Bill Keys drifted into the area about 1910 to take on the job as caretaker at the Desert Queen Mine, he naturally settled at this nearest source of water.

Alias Bill Keys

Judging from the early life of Bill Keys, there was little to indicate that he would take root, homestead, and remain in the canyon the rest of his long life. Born George Barth on September 27, 1879 in the little village of Palisade on the banks of Stinking Water Creek in Nebraska, he ran away from home at age 15. Later he changed his name to Bill Key when he joined Teddy Roosevelt's Rough Riders in 1898. (The "s" was tacked onto the end of Barth's adopted last name at a much later date to avoid confusion with John Kee, another pioneer rancher of the local area.) Due to illness, he did not participate in the fighting in Cuba. Upon his discharge he wandered west, working as a cowhand, deputy sheriff and bodyguard before taking up mining.

Death Valley Days

It was while developing his own claims in Death Valley's Funeral Range that Keys formed his life-long friendship with Walter Scott, who later achieved everlasting fame as Death Valley Scotty - a friendship that led to Bill's involvement in the notorious "Battle of Wingate Pass."

This was long before Scott had tapped his greatest mine in the person of Albert Johnson, the Chicago financier who later bankrolled many of Scotty's exploits and was the real builder of the incongruous Scotty's Castle in Death Valley. Walter Scott, a former Buffalo Bill Wild West star, was just another wandering prospector, though more flamboyant than most.

The "Battle of Wingate Pass" arose as the result of Scott finding himself in the embarrassing position of having to show his mine to his Eastern backers. Mark Twain once described a mine as "a hole in the ground owned by a liar". He may not have had Walter Scott specifically in mind, but it's a fact that Scott most definitely did not want his backers to see his worthless hole in the ground. The plot he hatched to avoid doing so came right out of his Wild West Show days.

There are several versions of the confrontation that took place in March of 1906 at the southern portal of Death Valley, but all agree that Bill Keys was among the men whom Scotty arranged to stage a mock ambush of the inspection party sent out to verify Scott's "rich" mine. Plenty of shots were fired and it had the desired effect of frightening off the Eastern tenderfoots. The only casualty was Scotty's brother Warner, who was accidentally wounded by an errant bullet. Later, Scotty and Keys were arrested over the incident but never brought to trial. Warner Scott fully recovered, and photographs showing him visiting Keys at the Desert Queen Ranch attest to their continuing friendship in later years.

Bill Keys, on the right, posed with Alfred MacArthur, one of the men sent out by Eastern backers who discovered that Death Valley Scotty's rich mine existed only in Scotty's imagination. (photo circa 1908, courtesy JTNP)

Making a Life

After the Wingate Pass affair, Keys drifted through other mining districts, finally arriving at Twentynine Palms about 1910. The McHaney Gang had by now abandoned the Desert Queen mill and Keys took up residency there while working as superintendent-caretaker at the Desert Queen Mine. By 1917, as an inscription on the main ranch house chimney indicates, he had begun his life work of developing the Desert Queen Ranch.

In one of his rare forays into Los Angeles to purchase mining equipment, Keys wandered into the Broadway Department Store and struck up the acquaintance of a saleswoman, Francis May Lawton. By 1918 they were married and the bride installed in her new canyon home. It was not to be an easy life, especially for one used to the conveniences of city life, but Mrs. Keys not only adapted to the desert, she thrived on it. While her husband busied himself with cattle-raising, mining activities, road building, plowing and other heavy labor, Mrs. Keys, later aided by the children, canned fruit and vegetables, milked cows and goats, cooked hearty meals for a growing brood, tended the garden and took care of the laundry - all of course without modern appliances or even the electricity to run them. With over 50 miles of rutted dirt roads separating the ranch from the nearest center of civilization, she of necessity provided services to her family that most of us take for granted: barber, doctor, nurse, and teacher.

The Keys family in the 1930s. (photo courtesy JTNP)

By 1932, in response to the growing educational needs of the children, Bill Keys erected a small schoolhouse and hired an instructor. Subsequently, when surrounding homesteaders began sending their children to the ranch, the county took over the responsibility for the Desert Queen School. The teacher's cabin and the tiny schoolhouse with its old-fashioned desks remain intact on the ranch grounds today.

The operation of ore-crushing mills, several of which remain on the ranch, was an important enterprise for Keys. Not only did it directly supplement his modest ranch income, it also enabled him to make the acquaintance of most of the miners of the Joshua Tree area. Through these customers Keys became aware of claims that had recently become abandoned. Always quick to take advantage of these situations, Keys eventually laid claim to over 35 mine and mill sites, some at great distances from the ranch. One of his main purposes in taking over an abandoned claim was the salvage of useful equipment left on the site by the prior operators. A great deal of machinery was brought back and incorporated into the Desert Queen Ranch where it remains for the visitor to discover, but most of it was sold for cash. Yet another source of income came from the leasing of some of the more promising claims.

In the canyon behind the ranch house, Keys constructed a large concrete dam. When full it held enough water to supply the needs of the ranch for several years. In winter the Keys children ice-skated on the lake; in summer it served as the old swimming hole as well as a source of fresh fish that had been stocked when the dam was built. Pipes led from the dam to a garden that had been enriched by hauling in soil from other areas. The pear trees still growing around the garden plot were planted after first loosening the hard native soil with dynamite.

Bill Keys loading his burro for a prospecting foray. (photo courtesy JTNP)

Water was a critical commodity for cattle as well as for people and gardens. Keys worked at building dams to create new or enhance existing natural catchments to provide water for his stock on an all-year basis. Water hole disputes soon arose between Keys and larger cattle operators, culminating in 1929 when Keys shot and wounded Homer Urton, a cowboy riding for C.O. Barker. This incident added to a growing legend that Bill Keys was a "bad hombre" and a man to be avoided.

But as local residents continued to build up Keys' reputation as a quick-tempered gun-fighter, a few outsiders found him to be a generous host and willing worker. Joshua Tree National Monument was established in 1936, completely encircling the Desert Queen Ranch. Although Keys was to have his conflicts with the Park Service, he was reported by the Superintendent of Joshua Tree to be dependable and honest. Dr. Edmund Jaeger, the famed dean of desert biologists, often visited the Desert Queen Ranch, feeling so warmly towards its owners that he named a newly discovered wildflower the Keysia, "in honor of Mr. and Mrs. Wm. Keys. . . whose perennial kindness is known to so many desert travelers."

Gunplay and Prison

The "bad man" legend surrounding Bill Keys would almost certainly have faded away had it not been for the intrusion of a new neighbor, who from the very beginning seemed intent on provoking an act of violence.

Worth Bagley had served as a deputy sheriff in Los Angeles, where he had developed a reputation for mistreating prisoners in his charge at the Los Angeles County Jail. It may have happened that rival cattlemen, aware of Bagley's penchant for violence, deliberately steered Bagley into homesteading a piece of property adjacent to Keys. From 1940 to 1943, tensions between the two men grew to the breaking point. Finally, on May 11, 1943 the inevitable clash took place; a gunfight in the tradition of the Old West in which Worth Bagley paid the ultimate price. Keys turned himself over to the authorities, confident he would soon be vindicated and be back at work on the ranch. But it was not to be that simple.

The gun duel had occurred in a lonely piece of desert, witnessed only by silent Joshua trees. According to Keys, he was driving back to his ranch from an outlying well on a road passing over part of Bagley's property, a road Keys had constructed and consistently used since long before Bagley had purchased the land. Coming to a cardboard sign propped up in the center of the road, he stopped to read its ominous message: "KEYS, THIS IS MY LAST WARNING. STAY OFF MY PROPERTY."

Keys walked ahead to a slight rise from which he discerned Bagley in the distance moving toward him, revolver in hand. By the time Bagley fired on him, Bill had returned to his idling vehicle and was in the process of retrieving his rifle. Three rapid shots dropped his assailant to the ground. Fearing a trick, Keys did not approach the body. He realized that he might be detained away from the ranch for a few days to account for his actions, so he went on to repair a pump necessary to keep his cattle watered before driving into Twentynine Palms to report the event to the proper authorities.

Investigators found Bagley dead, still clutching his revolver from which one shot had been fired. No footprints other than Bagley's were found in the soft sand around the body. In disregard of this evidence and relying instead on a deputy sheriff's opinion that Bagley had been shot in the back while in a kneeling posture, the court sentenced Keys to 12 years in prison on a charge of manslaughter. Bill Keys discovered, as have many men of independent ways, that the price of that independence can be the making of powerful enemies. Did certain cattle interests influence the course of the investigation and trial? We may never know for sure, but it is certain that important evidence was overlooked and not presented at the trial.

Months dragged into years for Bill Keys in San Quentin Prison. Convicted at age 64, he might not be released until he was 76 years old. A lesser man might have crumpled up and died; Keys was of sterner stuff. The self-discipline required to survive and prosper on the desert was carried with him into the prison cell. He read voluminously, a luxury he had never had time for during his busy days on the ranch. He exercised daily and younger prisoners respected his wiry strength. Meanwhile, the Keys children grew up to pursue lives away from the ranch. Only Mrs. Keys remained in the lonely alcove, waiting patiently for the day her husband would return. Slowly the ranch fell into decay.

But in the outside world events were stirring that would eventually vindicate Bill Keys and set him free. Erle Stanley Gardner, creator of the Perry Mason mystery stories, along with several other attorneys, had taken up the Keys case in the "Court of Last Resort", a series of articles appearing in a popular men's magazine in which cases of miscarriage of justice were brought before the public and officials in an attempt to obtain redress. Gardner had been acquainted with Keys since 1927 from camping trips into the Joshua Tree area. The publicity generated by Gardner undoubtedly aided Keys, but it was the work of State Assemblyman Vernon Kilpatrick, and specifically the record of his interview with Worth Bagley's last wife, Isabelle Clark, that finally broke the case wide open.

According to Mrs. Clark's testimony, she had been Bagley's ninth wife. She had resided with her new husband on his ranch adjacent to the Desert Queen Ranch in 1940, but was not on the scene when the shooting took place three years later, having moved out when Bagley served divorce papers on her. She believed that Bagley had probably been responsible for the shooting of some of Keys' stock. Most importantly, she related how Bagley had told her that he would "get that old goat", referring to Keys, and furthermore she had on several occasions actually observed Bagley waiting to ambush Keys along the same section of road where the shoot-out finally occurred.

Worth Bagley's clearly demonstrated hostility toward Keys and his doubtful mental condition as revealed by Mrs. Clark's testimony, resulted in a parole for Keys in 1948 followed by a full pardon in 1956.

Bill and Frances Keys on the frozen reservoir behind the ranch house after Bill's release from prison. (photo courtesy JTNP

Epilogue

At age 69 and after five years in prison, Bill Keys returned to his wife and home in the rocky canyon; not to a quiet life of retirement, but to a resumption of his old active ways. In 1950 he completed the final addition to Barker Dam which he renamed Bighorn Dam. He and Mrs. Keys played hosts to increasing numbers of recreationists, operating the ranch as a semi-resort. Movie companies found the spectacular scenery of the surrounding desert to their liking and shot several films there. Bill Keys even found himself playing the role of an old prospector in a Disney film titled *The Wild Burro of the West.*

Frances May Keys, the city girl whom Bill Keys had brought to a desolate desert canyon, who converted the canyon into a warm home for her family, and who maintained her feminine qualities in spite of her coarse environment, passed away in 1963. Left alone except for an occasional ranch hand to help maintain the ranch, Keys' remaining years were quiet ones. Finally recognized as a Grand Old Man of the Desert, he was elected grand marshal for the town of Joshua Tree's annual pioneer parade, a role he played with great gusto. With the help of friends, he even resurrected his old Wall Street Mill in 1966.

The end arrived on June 28, 1969. Keys was laid to rest beside his wife and three of their children in the small family cemetery at the entrance to the canyon where he had spent most of his life. It seems only appropriate that each of the graves, including his own, is surmounted by a rough-hewn headstone quarried by the hands of Bill Keys, desert pioneer.

A more detailed description of the life of Bill Keys appears in Art Kidwell's *Ambush, The Story of Bill Keys*, Pioneer Publishing, 1979

Going to town in Bill Keys' Apperson Jackrabbit, although exciting for the children, must have been punishing to certain parts of the anatomy. (photo courtesy JTNP)

A fine outlook opened from the crest. Far to the west lay my brace of giants, San Jacinto and San Gorgonio, a sort of Gog and Magog. Behind and to the east was a jumble of brown ranges, with pale slips of desert showing here and there between them. To the north I looked out over the Mojave Desert, the twin sister of the Colorado, from this point a wilderness of mountains, arid, aerial, almost phantasmal. Beautiful, too, they were in their elemental solitude, their delicacy of tone, and most so in their air of mystery, their magnetic drawing on the imagination. "Come," they seemed to say, "we are waiting for you: have waited since eternity began."

J. Smeaton Chase
California Desert Trails, 1919

CHAPTER 12

THE KEYS VIEW ROAD

FEATURES: Cap Rock Nature Trail, Johnny Lang grave, Keys View (mile-high desert viewpoint).

The Keys View Road, leading southward from Cap Rock Junction through a dense forest of Joshua trees, climbs to the crest of the Little San Bernardino Mountains, where one of the greatest vistas in California awaits the visitor. The best time to go is in early morning before desert winds stir up the dust or the Los Angeles smog has crept over San Gorgonio Pass.

Cap Rock

Cap Rock, where the Keys View Road begins, is a monolithic dome adorned near its summit by a balanced, visor-shaped boulder appearing much like the bill on a baseball cap. On its south side, the Cap Rock Nature Trail (.3 mile round trip) circles a boulder outcrop where a rare cluster of ferns grows in the microhabitat created by a rocky overhang.

Johnny Lang's Grave

Two and a half miles south of Cap Rock Junction, in the heart of a Joshua tree forest, a dirt road branches to the left (east), leading to the Lost Horse Mine trailhead. Just before this turnoff, immediately west of the Keys View Road, is the grave of Johnny Lang, the prospector whose story is related along with the history of the Lost Horse Mine in Chapter 13.

Keys View

Continuing south, the pavement climbs upward to the crest of the range to end at the Keys View overlook. The gentle aspect of the Little San Bernardinos as perceived from the automobile approach from the north is in stark contrast to the southern slopes falling away beneath the viewpoint. These plunge thousands of feet to the floor of the Coachella Valley, a flat expanse stretching away for mile after mile to end abruptly against the precipitous wall formed by the distant San Jacinto and Santa Rosa mountain ranges. This huge depression is a graben, a gigantic block of the Earth's surface that has dropped between two parallel faults.

The most prominent mountain across the valley is San Jacinto Peak, its 10,804-foot summit towering over 9,000 feet above Palm Springs, vaguely discernible as a dark smudge at the base of the mountain. In winter and spring, long fingers of snow extend down San Jacinto's furrowed north face toward San Gorgonio Pass, gateway to the desert for millions of metropolitan residents.

To the right of San Gorgonio Pass rises 11,499-foot San Gorgonio Mountain, highest point in Southern California. If the atmosphere is clear, the lowest point in Southern California can be seen in the same field of view. The vague, burnished surface of the Salton Sea, over 200 feet below sea level, lies far off to the south, filling the southern extension of the Coachella Valley. An even more expansive view may be gained by hiking up the trailess ridge behind the viewpoint to Inspiration Point (unmarked), a half-mile distant.

Nearly two thousand feet below Keys View is the site of the Hidden Gold Mine, a prospect once owned by Bill Keys and the principal reason why Keys scraped out the original road in 1926. (Note: The mine ruins are insignificant, difficult to locate, and the return hike up the hardscrabble hillside is extremely strenuous.)

There never was any idle time in that mill. There was always something to do. It is a pity that Adam could not have gone straight out of Eden into a quartz mill, in order to understand the full force of his doom to "earn his bread by the sweat of his brow."

Mark Twain
Roughing It, 1871

CHAPTER 13

THE LOST HORSE MINE

FEATURES: Mine ruins reached by trail, desert viewpoint.

The Lost Horse Mine was the most successful operation of its kind in what is now Joshua Tree National Park. Most of the 9,000 troy ounces of gold processed from its ores was produced at the turn of the twentieth century in the first ten years of the mine's operation. The stabilized structure of the 10-stamp mill is today's primary attraction, but there are also several large cyanide settling tanks, a huge winch used on the main shaft, and the stone foundations of the village that blossomed here during the late 1890s.

Johnny Lang and the Legends of the Lost Horse

Like any good desert mine, the Lost Horse has its legends, in this case involving a prospector named Johnny Lang. Of the many stories of the mine's discovery, the following version, supposedly related by Lang to Bill Keys, seems as likely to resemble the truth as any.

Johnny Lang many years after the heyday of the Lost Horse Mine. (photo courtesy JTNP)

In 1893 Lang was encamped at Pinyon Well near the present Geology Tour Road in Pleasant Valley. His horse strayed and he tracked it northward on foot, finally arriving at McHaney's camp in the vicinity of the Desert Queen Ranch. There he had a brief run-in with Jim McHaney, being told by the latter in no uncertain terms that his horse was "no longer lost" and to "get with his own kind", referring to "Dutch" Frank Diebold, another man of German ancestry camped over at Witch Spring (near present day Ryan Campground).

Lang recognized a clear threat to his health and removed himself as requested, still on foot. Diebold welcomed the footworn prospector and revealed that he had just discovered a rich gold prospect but had been unable to monument a claim, having been chased off by McHaney's cowboys. Subsequently, Johnny and his father George inspected the find and purchased Diebold's discovery rights for one thousand dollars.

Now the problem of claim-marking fell to Johnny. Several times approaching cowboys prevented him from accomplishing the task. How could he ever work his claim if he was already having problems just getting claim monuments erected? The senior Lang provided the obvious solution; take on partners. Thus on the 29th of December, 1893, the Lost Horse Claim was officially registered with the names of George W. Lang, John Lang, Ed Holland, and James J. Fyfe appearing as locators.

In 1895 the partners, except for Johnny Lang, sold their interests to the Ryan brothers, Thomas and J.D. "Jep", and development of the mine began in earnest. Jep Ryan transported a 10-stamp mill from the Colorado River, erected it on the site, and installed a water line from Lost Horse Well (formerly Witch Spring) where the Ryans had homesteaded a ranch. The years 1896-99 represented the peak production period for the mine. During this time, heavy gold ingots were concealed in a freight wagon and hauled out to Indio. No thieves ever caught on to this simple ploy. Up to 25 men were employed at the mine and mill, while a crew of 10 scoured the surrounding countryside for wood to fuel the steam engine powering the mill. The work crews were housed and fed in a little village of stone and wooden shacks located on the slope opposite the mill site.

Road agents may have ignored the bullion leaving the mine, but thievery of another sort was occurring before the gold was converted into ingot form. The primary product of the refining process used at the Lost Horse Mine was the amalgam, a lump of quicksilver containing dissolved amounts of gold from which the pure gold could later be separated. Jep Ryan's suspicions were aroused when the quantity of amalgam produced by the night shift, supervised by Johnny Lang, started running consistently smaller than Ryan's day shift. The mystery of the missing amalgam was solved when Ryan hired a man to hide in the mill and observe the night shift operation. Lang was discovered stealing part of the amalgam. When Ryan confronted Lang with the evidence and a choice - go to jail or sell out to the Ryans for $12,000 - Lang sold.

Within a few years a fault was encountered at a depth of 500 feet and the gold vein was lost. Attempts to relocate the ore body by drifts, or side tunnels, proved fruitless. The last major activity at the site occurred in 1936 when Jep Ryan re-processed 600 tons of tailings using the highly efficient cyanide process.

What of Johnny Lang? After accepting Jep Ryan's generous offer for his share of the Lost Horse, he removed himself to an abandoned cabin in a canyon (now bearing Lang's name) a few miles west of Hidden Valley. There Lang worked his Sulphide-Bismuth Claim, crushing the ore in a small arrastra. Years later, when the Lost Horse operation was deserted, he returned to the scene of his earlier transgressions to take up residence in the kitchen shack. Lang also resided for a short time at Bill Keys' Desert Queen Ranch. Because of Johnny's reputation for pilfering, Keys never allowed the old-timer to approach the ranch's ore-milling machinery. The prospector's brief stay at the ranch ended one night when he accidentally set fire to his tent residence.

As the years passed, Lang would occasionally sell Keys considerable quantities of gold, up to $900 worth at a time (at $32 a troy ounce). Keys always felt that Johnny's little arrastra and mine in Lang Canyon never produced such amounts of gold; Lang must have been tapping the amalgams he had hidden away during his glory days at the Lost Horse Mine.

When Lang's health and eyesight began to fail, he could no longer shoot C.O. Barker's cattle, which had sustained him for years, so he tied his four burros near his cabin and shot and ate them one by one. On January 10, 1925, Bill Keys and a companion found a note tacked on Lang's shack stating that the old prospector was going to town for supplies and would soon return. He never did. Three months later, Keys, Jeff Peeden and Frank Kiler, working on the construction of the Keys View Road, discovered the partly mummified remains of Johnny

Lang. The combination of the long walk out from the Lost Horse Mine, Lang's state of malnutrition, and the coldness of a winter night (the body was still wrapped in a thin canvas sleeping bag) had carried the old miner off to his final prospecting trip.

The authorities instructed Keys to bury the body where it was found. The grave may be seen today just west of the Keys View Road, a hundred feet north of the junction with the Lost Horse Mine road.

View of Malapai Hill and Pleasant Valley from the hillcrest behind the Lost Horse Mine.

Visiting the Lost Horse Mine

The trailhead for the Lost Horse Mine is located at the end of a short dirt road that turns off the Keys View Road 2.5 miles south of Cap Rock Junction. Since turnaround space is limited, vehicles towing trailers should not drive in. The 3.6-mile round trip hike to the mine itself is not strenuous, however this trip is best avoided in hot weather as neither water nor shade will be encountered.

The trail, which is really the old mine road, ascends the left side of the wash just beyond the road barricade, and can be easily followed to the fold high up on Lost Horse Mountain where the mine is located. In addition to the mine ruins, a sweeping view of the southern end of Queen Valley, Malapai Hill (a volcanic remnant), and Pleasant Valley may be gained by hiking the short distance to the crest of the hill above the mill site.

A different route, more scenic than the old mine road, goes directly up the wash from the parking area. This little canyon should be called "Nolina Gulch" because of the preponderance of these picturesque yucca-like plants, some growing to 10 feet in height at this locale. (The *Nolina bigelovii* is not a yucca. In spring some of the plants send up tall flower stalks of unusual beauty. The stalks of the male plants exhibit a feathery appearance, while those of the female plant become laden with attractive clusters of winged seed pods.) The first part of the canyon is narrow and partly shaded by overhanging pinyon pine branches. In about half a mile the rock walls are replaced by open slopes where a left-hand fork of the wash should be followed up a moderate slope to intersect the mine road. Turn right on the road and follow it the remaining distance to the mine. (Note: A number of dangerous shafts have been filled in by the Park Service but hazardous open pits and tunnels still remain; they should be approached only with the utmost caution and never entered.)

I had already learned how hard and long and dismal a task it is to burrow down into the bowels of the earth and get out the coveted ore; and now I learned that the burrowing was only half the work; and that to get the silver out of the ore was the dreary and laborious other half of it. We had to turn out at six in the morning and keep at it till dark. This mill was a six-stamp affair, driven by steam. Six tall, upright rods of iron, as large as a man's ankle, and heavily shod with a mass of iron and steel at their lower ends, were framed together like a gate, and these rose and fell, one after the other, in a ponderous dance, in an iron box called a "battery." Each of these rods or stamps weighed six hundred pounds. One of us stood by the battery all day long, breaking up masses of silver-bearing rock with a sledge and shoveling it into the battery. The ceaseless dance of the stamps pulverized the rock to powder, and a stream of water that trickled into the battery turned it to a creamy paste. The minutest particles were driven through a fine wire screen which fitted close around the battery, and were washed into . . . amalgamating pans. . . A quantity of quicksilver was kept always in the battery, and this seized some of the liberated gold and silver particles and held on to them; quicksilver was shaken in a fine shower into the pans, also, about every half hour, through a buckskin sack. Quantities of coarse salt and sulphate of copper were added, from time to time, to assist the amalgamation by destroying base metals which coated the gold and silver and would not let it unite with the quicksilver. All these tiresome things we had to attend to constantly. . .

At the end of the week the machinery was stopped and we "cleaned up". That is to say, we got the pulp out of the pans and batteries, and washed the mud patiently away till nothing was left but the long accumulating mass of quicksilver, with its imprisoned treasures. This we made into heavy, compact snow-balls, and piled them up in a bright luxurious heap for inspection. Making these snow-balls cost me a fine gold ring - that and ignorance together; for the quicksilver invaded the ring with the same facility with which water saturates a sponge - separated its particles and the ring crumbled to pieces.

Mark Twain
Roughing It, 1871

Early in the day when the senses are keen and fresh, take to climbing the mountains. The higher you climb, the more marvelous is the prospect. The country now acquires new importance, and every mountain range seen in the distance invites exploration.

Edmund C. Jaeger
The California Deserts, 1933

CHAPTER 14

AROUND RYAN MOUNTAIN

FEATURES: Ryan Campground, early cemetery, Headstone Rock, Indian Cave, Ryan Mountain Trail.

The whaleback of Ryan Mountain was named for the owners of the Lost Horse Mine, Thomas and Jep Ryan, brothers who took up a homestead at Lost Horse Well at the western base of the mountain in order to secure a reliable water source for their mine operation. The old Ryan Ranch has been abandoned to the elements and vandals for some years. The main ranch house burned in 1978, an unfortunate loss, for this structure was constructed for the Ryans around the turn of the twentieth century by Sam Temple, the model for the murderer of Juan Alessandro in Helen Hunt Jackson's famous novel *Ramona*.

A Pioneer Graveyard

Death and decay seem to pervade the old Ryan homestead. Within sight of the skeleton-like walls of the old ranch buildings are at least eight graves, scattered among the boulders and Joshua trees, some only faintly outlined by a ring of rocks with a larger cobble serving as a headstone. A few are denoted by the year of death painted on an adjacent boulder; only two are identified by name. The one marked "James" is the last resting place of Frank L. James, murdered in 1894 so that Jim McHaney could confiscate the Desert Queen Mine (see Chapter 16). Next to James is "Lopes", perhaps one of five Mexican miners who, according to legend, killed each other in a brawl and were buried in this makeshift cemetery.

The grave sites are only a short walk from Ryan Campground. From the east side of the campground proceed on foot across the open flats to the east, passing around the right (south) side of Headstone Rock, the prominent monolith precariously balanced on top of a rockpile about 100 yards distant. About 150 yards beyond Headstone Rock, continuing in the same general direction from the campground, is another cluster of low-lying boulders at the entrance to the old Ryan Ranch. The graves are located around the northern end of this outcrop.

A large boulder near the entrance to the old Ryan Ranch homestead marks the last resting place of Lopes (Lopez?) (1894) and Frank L. James (1893).

Ryan Mountain and Indian Cave

In contrast to the spectral remains of the old Ryan Ranch, the 3-mile round-trip hike up Ryan Mountain is a reaffirmation of life. The pulse accelerates, the senses become more acute, and one may renew the acquaintance of lungs and muscles previously taken for granted. The view from the summit is one of the grandest in the park, perhaps made more so because it demands more effort than pushing on a gas pedal. In morning and late afternoon, when the shadows begin to lengthen, or on a summer night beneath a full moon, the surrounding desert reveals its greatest splendors to those who make the ascent.

The Ryan Mountain Trail begins at a parking area next to the park highway approximately ¼-mile west of the Sheep Pass Group Campground turnoff. At the west end of the parking area is Indian Cave, a natural rock shelter that was used as a work site by the aboriginal inhabitants as proven by the presence of bedrock mortars and grinding slicks, these latter being smooth, flat faces worn on rock surfaces from repeated seed-grinding operations.

The Geology Tour Road leads southward from Queen Valley on gently rolling terrain accented by extensive stands of Joshua trees. As the road approaches Squaw Tank, the brooding mass of Malapai Hill and an oddly-shaped balanced rock (below) will be seen off to the right (west).

In the desert you contemplate earth and time and life. You see the obituary column of the circling vultures, and also the miracle of dawn light catching against thorns and producing halos.

You find perspective. . .

And peace. . .

Ruth Kirk
Desert, The American Southwest, 1973

CHAPTER 15

QUEEN VALLEY AND THE GEOLOGY TOUR ROAD

FEATURES: Queen Valley Joshua tree forest, self-guiding geology tour, Malapai Hill, Squaw Tank, Gold Coin Mine, Pleasant Valley, Pinyon Well.

Queen Valley

Queen Valley, where the Geology Tour Road begins, is one of the author's favorite haunts. Bounded on the north by the craggy ramparts of Queen Mountain (displaying a prominent landslide scar created by a severe summer downpour in 1946), the broad, flat floor of the valley expands mile after mile southward to the imperceptible divide separating it from Pleasant Valley. The 4000-foot elevation, combined with the valley's well-drained alluvial soil, creates an ideal habitat for the thousands of Joshua trees stretching out to the horizon. Some of the finest tree yucca specimens in the park crowd the highway between Sheep Pass and Jumbo Rocks Campground. The largest of these is "Elmer's Tree" (1.6 miles east of Sheep Pass, 2.7 miles west of Jumbo Rocks), named after Elmer Camp, an early-day park employee who would park beneath the tree during thunderstorms to watch for lightning-caused fires. Queen Valley is also one of the few places in the park where the brilliant crimson blossoms of the Mojave mound cactus (*Echinocereus mojavensis*) may be seen from the car. A few scattered clumps appear on the north side of the park highway immediately west of Elmer's Tree. Look for their blossoms in April and May.

Malapai Hill and Squaw Tank

The Geology Tour Road turns southward off the highway near the eastern end of Queen Valley. The dirt road is normally maintained in good condition. Round trip distance from the highway to Pleasant Valley and back is approximately 18 miles. The Geology Tour Guide is dispensed from a container at the turnoff and explains, through numbered posts along the route, the geology of this part of the park. Taken at a leisurely pace, this loop consumes at least 2 hours. Pit toilets and interesting rock formations at Squaw Tank make this site a good destination for a picnic.

The tour road first traverses several miles of open country, gradually climbing to the crest of a divide before descending through boulder outcrops to Pleasant Valley. On the approach to Squaw Tank, the black cone of Malapai Hill, a basaltic remnant of an unborn volcano, looms up on the right. The brooding bulk looks larger than it really is, and the scramble to the top, which commands a superb view, is not as difficult as it first appears. Sturdy footgear, preferably boots, are a must. A good starting point for the climb is at Post #7. A much easier stroll from this same point can be made to a large balanced rock that is particularly noticeable from farther down the road at Squaw Tank. From Post #7 it is visible at ground level several hundred yards to the southwest.

The picturesque rock formations at Squaw Tank.

The Squaw Tank Picnic Area is located at the edge of prominent quartz monzonite outcrops on the east side of the tour road. Indians were attracted to this site by the water that often stood in the canyon to the southeast. A fine bedrock mortar, worked by the women of Squaw Tank, is located on the rock apron at the base of the rockpile immediately adjacent to the parking area. An early desert traveller described Squaw Tank much as it must have appeared when only Indians knew of this remote and desolate site.

> In a pile of rock that I skirted I had been told I should find one of those natural tanks of water (*tinaja* is the common Spanish word) on which the desert traveller often has to place precarious trust - precarious because they are

mere rain catchments. This one is known as Squaw Tanks. I easily found the place, being led to it by my nose. A small quantity of slimy liquid remained, nauseous with putrefying bodies of birds, rats and lizards. A man perishing of thirst might have brought himself to drink it, but would probably not have survived the draught. It was no disappointment to me, for my canteens were newly filled, but the incident had a moral for me, nevertheless. (J. Smeaton Chase, *California Desert Trails*, 1919)

Beginning in the late 19th century, cattlemen were drawn to the lush grasslands of Pleasant Valley and it was they who raised the small dam at the catchment that Chase found so repulsive. Their barrier no longer retains water and is now just another reminder of how man attempted to bend the desert to his desires - in the end the desert was victorious.

Gold Coin Mine and Pleasant Valley

From Squaw Tank the road skirts a ridge extending from the Hexie Mountains, drops down to the clay playa of Pleasant Valley, and there makes a one-way circuit, taking in the Gold Coin Mine and the entrance to Pinyon Well before closing on itself again. WARNING: If there has been wet weather or the playa appears muddy, it is best to turn around rather than risk miring in a quagmire.

At the point where the tour road makes a sharp bend to the south are the ruins of the Gold Coin Mine. Discovered in 1900, the Gold Coin was operated by the American-German Mining Company until as late as 1938. It is a good place to park the car and survey the country on foot. From behind the rusting tanks and concrete mill foundation at the lower mine works, an abandoned road leads up the mountainside, passing a number of tunnels and shafts pockmarking the slope. The road soon disappears but by then the hiker has climbed high enough to obtain an unobstructed view of Pleasant Valley. Traces of roads criss-cross the valley floor. All of them, including the tour road, are visible reminders of the gold mining era, when every bite of food, piece of machinery, plank of lumber, and even the water used at the mines were hauled by the heavy wagons that followed these rough thoroughfares. Routes from Indio into the Joshua Tree region entered and crossed over the barrier of the Little San Bernardino Mountains by way of Fargo, Berdoo, and Pushawalla canyons to converge in Pleasant Valley. From here routes exited north to Queen Valley and east either to Eldorado Canyon or via Fried Liver Wash to Pinto Basin.

Another feature best observed from the elevation above the Gold Coin Mine deserves mention because it is responsible for the viewpoint itself. Almost due west is a distinctive notch in the skyline of the Little San Bernardinos known as The Blue Cut. Its color is derived from a bluish-colored granodiorite mineral exposed by movement of the Blue Cut Fault, a lateral slippage which over the eons has offset one side of the fault 12 miles relative to the other side. The south slopes of the Hexies, where the Gold Coin Mine is located, are another manifestation of the same fault, only in addition to lateral slippage, the north side of the fault has recently been thrust upward, creating the fresh, steep slopes of the Hexie Mountains.

Thousands of barrel cacti have colonized these precipitous slopes, their great numbers not obvious except in morning or late afternoon when the slanting rays of the sun shine through and illuminate their colorful barbs. Then they stand like a holy army, each soldier encased by his protective glowing halo.

The ruins of the Gold Coin Mine provide an excellent view of Pleasant Valley and the Little San Bernardino Mountains. The Geology Tour Road, like most by-ways in the park, follows a trail blazed by early teamsters driving rigs like the one shown below. (photo courtesy JTNP)

Pinyon Well

After the Gold Coin, the tour road crosses the playa and arrives at a road junction. The left fork leads to Berdoo Canyon and is normally impassable to passenger cars. The tour road continues to the right, snaking along the base of the mountains until it reaches the mouth of a small canyon (Post #15). Visitors can park here for the pleasant stroll to the site of Pinyon Well, 0.8 mile up-canyon.

As early as 1890 two prospectors from Indio - Al Tingman and Ed Holland - had established themselves at Pinyon Well and constructed a primitive arrastra to extract gold from ore hauled from their nearby mines. By 1895 a two-stamp mill, operated by either "Dutch" Frank Diebold or the Tingman/Holland partnership, was in operation. (This small mill was probably running a year or so earlier, since ore from both the Lost Horse and Desert Queen mines, discovered in 1893 and 1894 respectively, was initially transported to Pinyon Well for processing.) Certainly by 1895 the well had been excavated in place of the original spring at the site. With the development of a dependable water supply, teamsters began utilizing the Pushawalla Canyon - Pinyon Well route.

It is difficult to imagine that a little village once existed in the narrow canyon at Pinyon Well. George Wharton James, traveling through this settlement near the turn of the twentieth century, re-corded his impressions: "There are a few cabins and a stamp mill sit-uated in a cozy nook in the mountains, and - pleasing face - the homes of families, where the voices of women and children are heard."

The little two-stamper at Pinyon Well was a center of local activity one hundred years ago. (photo courtesy JTNP)

On the desert any water supply was eyed with envy by the chronically water-short mines. In 1912-13 the New Eldorado Mining Company installed a 9-mile pipeline leading from Pinyon Well to the mine site at the western edge of Pinto Basin. It operated intermittently until the last mining activities in the early 1930s. The presence of this water line may explain why developers bought up the available land in Pleasant Valley and attempted to subdivide it in the 1920s. Had there been sufficient water, the Pleasant Valley Freeway might be circumnavigating the downtown business district today instead of the Geology Tour Road making its quiet circuit.

Walking up-canyon to Pinyon Well, one can almost hear the sounds of heavy wagons creaking along, mules and horses straining under their loads, with the constant thumping of the stamp mill growing steadily louder. At last one turns a corner, to be greeted by silent ruins - a couple of cement tanks, a faint platform upon which a cabin once stood, a few bits of rusting pipe. The laughter of children, the scolding of their mothers, the curses of dust-covered teamsters and sweating mill operators, have echoed off the rock walls of the canyon to disappear into a lost era.

At the mouth of the canyon leading to Pinyon Well, the tour road turns back toward Squaw Tank to complete its transit. This last stage passes through a stand of exceptionally large holy-cross or pencil cholla (*Opuntia ramosissima*). Normally attaining heights of 3 to 5 feet, some of these monsters grow to 8 feet or more in this area.

Bedrock mortar at Squaw Tank.

Accursed greed for gold,
To what dost thou not drive the heart of man?

Virgil, Aeneid , 30 B.C.

CHAPTER 16

THE DESERT QUEEN MINE

FEATURES: Extensive mine workings, pinyon-juniper woodland.

Clinging to a cliff overlooking a narrow ravine a few miles north of Jumbo Rocks Campground, the workings of the Desert Queen Mine are among the most impressive in the park. They are reached via a short dirt access road that turns off the park highway opposite the Geology Tour Road. From the parking area the old mine road leads eastward a quarter-mile to the mine site. The stone foundations of several buildings are encountered before arriving at the shafts, tunnels, and rusting machinery of the mine proper.

The huge waste dumps spilling down the steep, boulder-strewn slopes offer concrete evidence of the great enterprise that was the Desert Queen Mine. In contrast, the mine's history is shrouded in uncertain legend. Like a typical dime-novel Western, it begins with murder.

Abandoned machinery - Desert Queen Mine.

Murder and the McHaneys

In the spring of 1894 a 35 year-old miner named Frank L. James was employed at the recently discovered Lost Horse Mine. In his spare time he scoured the surrounding countryside in search of a lode for himself, one day returning to his cabin in possession of some exceptionally rich gold ore. Naturally this set the little camp at the Lost Horse to buzzing. Word of James' discovery soon reached the ears of the notorious Jim McHaney, leader of a cattle-rustling gang headquartered in the nearby Hidden Valley area. As the legend goes, McHaney ordered his men to follow James to his claim and there dispose of the hapless miner. What is definitely known from the coroner's report is that on April 5, 1894, Frank L. James was killed, the result of two pistol shot wounds inflicted by Charles Martin. The Riverside Daily Enterprise recorded Martin's version:

> He [Martin] left San Bernardino about six weeks ago with a grubstake from Byron Waters to prospect on the desert north of Indio. On Monday, April 2nd, he located a quartz claim, which is supposed to be quite rich. Two days later James located the whole or a part of the same ground. The day the killing occurred, Martin met James on the claim in the presence of Messrs. Myer and McHaney. James asked Martin, pointing to a monument, if it was his. He replied in the affirmative, whereupon James said, "You go and tear it down or I will cut your heart out."
>
> Martin replied: "I will not tear the monument down and you will not cut my heart out."
>
> At that James made a lunge at Martin with a knife. He cut him on the left arm near the shoulder. . . . Martin had no weapon and was guarding against the cutting with his left hand.
>
> A gun belonging to one of the other men was lying on the ground several feet back of where the men were struggling. As James kept advancing with the knife, Martin grabbed the gun and shot while he was advancing. This did not stop him and another shot was fired, taking effect in James' breast and killing him. The miners in the locality then congregated, examined into all the circumstances and the meeting concluded to bury the body owing to the heat of the desert and the long distance to the railroad.

Why James would be so foolish as to attempt a knife attack on a man who was accompanied by two friends, and why there happened to be a pistol conveniently deposited on the ground within reach of Martin was never explained. As there were no witnesses other than McHaney and Myer, the inquest jury acquitted Martin on the grounds of self-defense. The unfortunate Mr. James was buried near the old Ryan Ranch where his grave may still be seen (Chapter 14).

Two versions are told of Jim McHaney's subsequent payoffs to his partners in crime. According to Bill Keys, the pioneer homesteader who became an intimate friend of Bill McHaney (the good McHaney brother), Martin simply received $4,700 in cash, while Myer was delegated the right to run cattle at Cow Camp north of Barker Dam.

The second version, as related by early Twentynine Palms resident Maud Carico Russell, is more interesting because it involves the wrath of a woman. It seems the McHaneys installed their sister Carrie

Harrington as a partner in the Desert Queen Mine (the name they bequeathed to their ill-gotten lode). Myer was left out, presumably minding his cattle at Cow Camp, and Martin was a silent partner, the sister's share of the mine profits reverting to him as hush money. Sister Carrie, feeling she was on the short end of the deal, became so enraged that one day she picked up a gun and ran the feared Jim McHaney out of camp. She later encouraged the Bank of Zambro to foreclose on the mine.

During the two years the McHaneys were in possession, the Desert Queen produced a modest fortune, a sum between $27,000 and $40,000 according to Bill Keys. A good percentage of this must have come from the "Rat's Nest", a rich pocket of ore that Bill McHaney claimed to have discovered. Perhaps it was this ore that fueled the statement of the State Mineralogist in his Annual Report of 1896: "Some of the quartz has been so rich in gold as to cause the most extravagant reports of the value of the mine."

The profits from the Desert Queen ran like water through the fingers of Jim McHaney. In a wild spree he tried to do "Diamond Jim" Brady one better by sporting diamonds on his hat band, belt and cane, as well as on rings for his fingers. By 1896, falling production and his wastrel ways finally caught up with him. The bank foreclosed on the mine and the McHaney brothers went their separate ways - Jim continuing his wayward existence until he was sent to prison for counterfeiting, and Bill to the free life of a prospector on the high desert around Twentynine Palms.

Keys Takes Control

In 1910 William Morgan, an elderly ex-mining engineer, purchased the Desert Queen Mine. About this same time William F. Keys drifted into the area and because of his experience in hard rock mining was hired as mine supervisor, watchman, and assayer - duties he performed from 1910 until Morgan's death in 1915. With Morgan's passing, Keys successfully pressed his claim to the Desert Queen based on the considerable back wages owed to him. Except for one incident, Keys apparently maintained control of the Desert Queen Mine over the next forty years, although he probably leased the mine occasionally. The one time Keys relinquished ownership provides another tale of the desert.

In the early 1930s a man named Frederick Brinton Morton purchased the Desert Queen Mine from Keys. Morton was a prominent Altadena jeweler and also a frustrated adventurer fascinated by stories of incredible wealth just waiting to be scooped from the ground. In 1931 Morton was approached by a Mr. Hapwell, who billed himself as an experienced mining engineer. In actuality Hapwell had roamed the desert mining camps as a cook and laborer long enough to pick up the appropriate prospector's lingo with which to convince the naive Morton of his qualifications.

All he required, insisted Hapwell, to turn the Desert Queen into a bonanza was a modest capital outlay. The reason why Keys wasn't rich by now was his lack of financial resources with which to properly develop the mine. Morton, of course, jumped at this golden opportunity. Forming a partnership with Hapwell, he purchased the mine from Keys for $50,000 of which Keys received a $6,000 down payment.

Quite by accident, the crew of miners hired by Hapwell soon struck a rich ore pocket. As might be guessed by now, the wily confidence man kept the discovery a secret from his partner in Altadena. The ore was processed using a two-stamp mill set up in a side canyon. After the pocket was exhausted, a convenient "cave-in" collapsed the access tunnel.

Meanwhile, as Morton's finances became drained, he began issuing stock in the Desert Queen without bothering to incorporate as required by the California Securities Law. Finally Morton could no longer meet the payroll, the mine was closed, and the broken jeweler was convicted of fraud. The honest but wise Bill Keys repossessed the mine he had sold only a short time before.

What of the "mining engineer" Hapwell? He and his wife, so poor at the start that Morton had to advance them money to buy their groceries, were reported to have taken a round-the-world trip before dropping out of sight.

The Desert Queen Mine as it appears today.

. . . in a dry country such as the American West the wounds men make in the earth do not quickly heal. Still, they are only wounds; they aren't absolutely mortal. Better a wounded wilderness than none at all.

Wallace Stegner
Coda: Wilderness Letter, 1960

It comes back to me that of all the places to camp, the desert is probably the friendliest.

Wallace Stegner
The Rediscovery of America, 1946

CHAPTER 17

JUMBO ROCKS AREA

FEATURES: Rock formations, Skull Rock Trail, Live Oak Tank, Ivanpah Tank, Split Rock.

Jumbo Rocks Campground

Imagine a vast array of rocks - balanced rocks, rock towers, stony buttes, walls and domes; rocks shaped like people, rocks resembling dinosaurs, rocks depicting goblins, ad infinitum. Mix well and toss into a heap covering several square miles of Joshua tree-studded desert and you have a fair approximation of the country surrounding Jumbo Rocks Campground.

Sooner or later, everyone who stays here succumbs to the desire to scramble over and through this natural jungle-gym. Campers with children rarely have trouble keeping the youngsters occupied. The agility of youth is not required, however, to gain a flavor of this rugged landscape by hiking the short nature trail connecting the campground with Skull Rock.

Skull Rock Interpretive Trail

The Skull Rock Trail originates off the main campground road in a flat a few yards beyond (but not on) the Loop D (Campfire Amphitheater) turnoff. Heading north out of the campground over a low rise, the trail wanders among big boulders and typical high desert vegetation, depositing the hiker at Skull Rock beside the park highway only a quarter mile distant from the starting point. Along the way, interpretive signs explain the plant life and geologic features.

Skull Rock

Skull Rock is the turnaround point for those without the ability or inclination to take on a little rock-scrambling and some tricky route-finding. From Skull Rock the trail continues for another mile and a quarter north across the highway where it enters an area of maze-like canyons, turns westward, and eventually emerges opposite the campground entrance road. Ducks (small piles of rocks stacked one on top of another) mark portions of the route, but the trail is indistinct and easy to miss at several points.

The rock formation known as the Pope's Hat overlooks the tree that gives Live Oak Tank its name.

Among the most noticeable features to be encountered are the aplite dikes caused by intrusion of a molten mineral into cracks formed in the surrounding solid rock. The aplite is lighter in color than the adjacent quartz monzonite. Because the quartz monzonite is much softer, it erodes away more rapidly, often leaving free-standing aplite "walls" reminiscent of the ruins of some ancient civilization.

This northern section of the Skull Rock Trail presents the opportunity to escape from all sights and sounds of human activity. Here the true essence of desert wilderness may be captured in solitude not available in the campground.

Live Oak and Ivanpah Tanks

Despite the apparent barrenness of the surrounding desert, the grasses and shrubs lightly cloaking the high desert can provide nutritious fodder for cattle. The key for successful cattle raising was water, which explains why cowboys working for C.O. Barker constructed two modest dams east of Jumbo Rocks in the early decades of the twentieth century. They are accessed by a dirt road turning south off the park highway 1.3 miles east of Jumbo Rocks Campground. After skirting a rock outcrop the road ends in 0.4 mile at a small parking area above the wash containing Live Oak Tank. (Warning: The road is narrow, with extremely limited turnaround space; vehicles towing trailers should not enter.)

From the end of the road the big tree that gives Live Oak Tank its name is easily discerned to the southeast at the base of a rock formation appropriately dubbed the Pope's Hat. One can easily visualize the days of the cattlemen when lazy steers could always be found reclined beneath the protective shade of the tree. The bovines had the right idea, and today's picnickers are often found emulating their behavior. The tree is a rare hybrid oak, a cross between the dwarf-like turbinella oak (*Quercus turbinella calif.*), common throughout the highlands of the park, and the valley oak (*Q. lobata*) which grows in the faraway San Joaquin Valley southward into Los Angeles County. Botanists have classified it as *Quercus x munzii* Tucker. Whatever its genetic heritage, the oak's shade has been a welcome surprise enjoyed by many a desert traveller.

Downstream from Live Oak Tank.

An easy one-mile loop hike to Ivanpah Tank via a beautiful desert wash may be made from Live Oak. A natural trail is provided by the smooth, sandy floor of the canyon leading downstream from the big oak. In a few paces the visitor will encounter the low stone wall that once retained a pool of water, the "tank" of Live Oak Tank. Now the primitive dam is filled to the brim with sand. Gradually the wash curves to the left (east), passing between rock walls decorated by handsome junipers. Farther on the canyon widens into an open flat, the former lakebed of Ivanpah Tank. Ivanpah's impressive dam has settled and cracked over the years until only a modest puddle forms in the wettest seasons, a wraith-like reminder of the considerable body of water retained in yesteryears.

The loop hike is completed by climbing the bluff overlooking the dam on the left (north) side. There, a trace of a dirt road leads back to the Live Oak Tank access road, which when followed back to Live Oak Tank completes the circumnavigation of the rock outcrop of which the Pope's Hat forms the western terminus.

More energetic hikers may elect to follow the wash below Ivanpah Tank. At first it passes through a narrow, winding defile, then in a quarter-mile opens up somewhat where a small concrete dam backs up a reservoir of sand. The inviting wash can lure the hiker on for miles. The best way to return is to backtrack to Ivanpah Tank and proceed from there as described above.

Ivanpah Tank

Split Rock

Split Rock is reached via the short, paved road that turns north off the park highway opposite the Live Oak Tank turnoff. A huge boulder, fractured neatly in two, gives this primitive picnic area its name. The back side of the rock is visible from the parking area, and the cool, overhanging north side is easily reached by walking a few paces on a pathway leading into the boulders. A small concrete dam is located in one of the recesses below Split Rock.

Split Rock

Since one knows intimately only the country he has walked over, take my hint: abandon the motor car as soon as possible and travel on foot. Then you will move in a leisurely manner, confine your wanderings to a small area, and enter into profitable intimacy with nature.

Edmund C. Jaeger
The California Deserts, 1933

CHAPTER 18

BELLE AND WHITE TANK CAMPGROUNDS

FEATURES: Bread Loaf Rock, Arch Rock Nature Trail, White Tank, Grand Tank.

Belle Campground

Belle Campground, situated 1.4 miles south of Pinto Wye, is one of the smaller and relatively undeveloped campgrounds in the park. Its spacious campsites, with ample room for parking, make it a popular destination for parties with several vehicles.

Belle has been a resting place for desert travellers for a long time. Teamsters hauling food and equipment to nearby mines often stopped

Bread Loaf Rock

at Belle, which they referred to as Castle Rock Cove. No doubt old-time prospectors such as Quartz Wilson, Johnny Lang, and Bill McHaney stopped here overnight to share a campfire and swap stories with the freight haulers. Perhaps these tall tales of mines and wealth lured one of the wagoners to abandon his rig and take up the quest for mineral riches. It could explain the reported 1978 sighting by an eleven year-old girl of an old, weathered wagon somewhere on the lower slopes of Belle Mountain, whose summit, crowned by communication towers, rises up behind the campground.

A more definite hiking objective is Bread Loaf Rock. The aptly named boulder is a pleasant picnic site (a shady overhang provides shelter from the sun). It is located about a quarter of a mile from the campground, behind the nearest rock outcrop to the northeast. The California Riding and Hiking Trail and a wide, sandy wash have to be crossed to reach the formation.

White Tank Campground

White Tank Campground, 1.8 miles south of Belle Campground, is also relatively undeveloped. Located on the edge of a wilderness of rocks, the campground provides unlimited opportunities for hiking and rock-scrambling. A short distance into this stony stronghold are two "tanks", further reminders of the days when cattlemen dammed up small natural catchments so they could graze their stock in the otherwise waterless terrain.

White Tank is the smaller and more easily located of the two. It was not named as one might think for its surroundings of light-colored rocks, but for a certain "Captain" White who was associated with the nearby Goldfields of America Mine. Mr. White is further

Arch Rock

immortalized by having his name attached to the type of rock responsible for the most spectacular landscapes in the park - Jumbo Rocks, Hidden Valley, Squaw Tank, Indian Cove, and the Wonderland of Rocks. At each of these locations the predominant rock is composed of the same minerals in the same ratios as specimens first analyzed from the White Tank area, implying their common origin. Geologists use the term "White Tank quartz monzonite" whenever they describe this particular mineral combination.

Just a few steps from the campground, White Tank provides a camper with shady solitude.

Set within a narrow, rock-ribbed canyon, White Tank is a good site for a picnic; there is cool shade on the warmest of days. But finding White Tank can be a bit of a challenge. The easiest route to describe is to follow the Arch Rock Trail, which starts near the center of the campground. At the northern end of the campground the trail turns eastward over a low hill and ends next to Arch Rock, which is viewed by stepping to the right into a pocket formed by a natural jointing in the rocks. White Tank lies directly south from here and can be found by following the joint pattern. This requires some climbing over boulders, keeping Arch Rock on the left. In a dozen yards the joint system descends into the rocky defile containing the sand-filled remains of White Tank. A cool, cavernous passage beneath house-sized boulders may be explored upstream from the small dam. Downstream, the first major tributary wash entering from the right provides an easier return route to the campground.

Grand Tank is located more deeply in the stony wilderness. It once contained a considerable body of water (up to 20 feet in depth) which supported colonies of fairy and tadpole shrimp. The ancestors of these minute crustaceans evidently made their way to this and other remote desert water holes on the feet of migrating waterfowl. A visit to Grand Tank entails an invigorating round trip hike of about 2 miles. Again the Arch Rock Trail is followed to its end, only instead of making a right turn at Arch Rock (as if going to White Tank), an informal continuation of the Arch Rock Trail is followed downslope to a dry stream bed and up the opposite slope where there is evidence of heavy foot traffic. Grand Tank is located farther on in this general direction. A rough sort of path leads, after a short boulder-scramble, into a rock alcove which is exited on the right via another short rock-climb. Thence an ill-defined pathway leads across gentler terrain to a spot overlooking Grand Tank.

The Grand Tank loop may be completed by following the wash below Grand Tank for about 5 minutes hiking time from the dam. Then the right-hand bank may be easily scaled and the campground reached by circling around to the right, crossing a few shallow washes en route.

Grand Tank in the days when it held water.

In this particular desert, the strong appeal to every lover of wild places lies in the very vastness of its broad, pebble-strewn and brush-covered basins, and in the surrounding bizarre, sere, and often barren but colorfully banded mountain ranges, which rise with remarkable steepness from the desert floor.

Edmund C. Jaeger
The North American Deserts, 1957

CHAPTER 19

PINTO BASIN

FEATURES: Archeological discoveries, mining ruins, Cholla Garden, Ocotillo Patch, sand dunes.

No feature in the park so dwarfs man as does Pinto Basin. Its sheer size, uncluttered by mankind's usual impedimenta, combines with the general barrenness of the valley's floor and starkness of the encircling mountains to create the penultimate desert environment. The effect is heightened by the presence of a low ridge of sand dunes bisecting the western part of the basin. One need only step a few paces from the highway to understand the dread that early travellers had of the desert, when a lame horse or broken wagon could mean a long, slow death. Yet a subtle beauty resides in the vast emptiness, the clear, pure air, and in the sounds of wind, birds and insects that interrupt what might otherwise be an oppressive silence. People have been attracted and repelled by Pinto Basin for a long, long time.

Pinto Man

The environment of Pinto Basin, stable and timeless as it may appear, has in reality changed drastically, even in the brief period since man first crossed the Bering Strait and filtered down into the Americas. Just a few thousand years ago what are now the deserts of North America experienced much greater amounts of rainfall. During this pluvial period a series of streams and lakes formed throughout the Great Basin, including parts of the Mojave Desert. Forests grew on the mountains ringing Pinto Basin, and a sluggish stream meandered through the center of the valley, slowly flowing from the western end to exit through the gap between the Eagle Mountains and the Coxcombs at the eastern extremity.

Perhaps as late as two to four thousands years ago a primitive people discovered this fertile valley and settled along the banks of the stream. They remained for a long period and then departed, leaving behind some of their characteristic stone tools and arrowpoints. There they lay until the early 1930s when they were discovered by Elizabeth Crozier Campbell*, a talented amateur archeologist residing in Twentynine Palms and associated with the Southwest Museum in Los Angeles. A preponderance of the recovered artifacts were tools used for hunting and are of such unique design that the terms "Pinto Man" and "Pinto Man Culture" have come to be used in describing this ancient race. In the years since the initial discovery in Pinto Basin, other Pinto Man sites, exhibiting identical types of artifacts, have been excavated at widely separated locations on the California deserts.

The Pinto Man site is located in an inaccessible region in the eastern part of Pinto Basin. Since it is a sensitive archeological area, it may be visited only under the supervision of the National Park Service.

Mining Activities

The western part of Pinto Basin exhibits signs of more recent human activity. Mines such as the Gold Point, Gold Fields of America, Silver Bell, Golden Bell, Golden Trumpet, Eldorado, Golden Bee, along with dozens of other prospects, are visible at various points along the park highway. Very little is known of their histories. Some were worked as early as the 1880s, others as recent as the start of World War II. Most were quickly scavenged for machinery and building materials as soon as they were abandoned, leaving only waste rock dumps, dangerous shafts and equally hazardous tunnels.

* Prior to her death in 1971, Ms. Campbell donated her extensive artifact collection, consisting of over 150,000 individual items, to Joshua Tree National Park.

The Silver Bell is one of the easiest mines to see from the road and visit on foot. From a small pullout beside the road 5.3 miles east from White Tank Campground (2.2 miles west from the Cholla Garden), the open cuts of the mine with its two wooden ore bins situated just below, can be observed about a half-mile to the south on the crest of the range of hills running parallel to the highway. To visit the site requires scrambling across a boulder-strewn wash to gain the old, eroded mine access road that appears as an obvious scar traversing the hillside. As usual, extreme caution should be exercised when examining this or any other abandoned mining operation.

Ruins of the Silver Bell Mine

Cholla Garden and the Ocotillo Patch

East of the Silver Bell, the highway bends around a hillock and enters the Cholla Garden. A short nature trail introduces visitors to what is surely the most respected of desert plants, *Opuntia bigelovii*, also known as the "Teddy Bear cholla" or "jumping cholla". J. Smeaton Chase described the stickery monster in most colorful prose:

> First it is in villainous traits and in the ill-regard of every desert traveller. It is an ugly object three or four feet high, with stubby arms standing out like amputated stumps. The older parts are usually black with decay, the rest a sickly greenish white, and the whole thing is covered with horrible barbed spines, uncountable in quantity and detestable in every regard. It has, moreover, a very vile habit of shedding its joints, and these roll by instinct into the places where they can most easily achieve their purpose, which is to stab the feet of horses and spike pedestrians through their boots, as they readily can do. Every one who has travelled with horses on the desert has had the job of ridding his animals of these devils, which in many places grow so thickly that to dodge them is out of the question. The Indians say they jump at you:

this sounds like an exaggeration, but upon my word I don't know. Often when I have felt sure that I passed clear of a certain cholla I found he had me after all. [*California Desert Trails, 1919*]

Caution is the word of the day when examining the cholla.

To most desert visitors the cholla is not as evil as Chase paints it. In morning and late afternoon, when backlit by the slanting rays of the sun, there is no more photogenic desert plant than "Bigelow's accursed cholla".

The loose cholla joints serve a useful purpose for at least one desert inhabitant, the packrat (*Neotoma*), who incorporates them into its nest for protection from predators. Frank Cole, first Superintendent of Joshua Tree National Monument, reported one method whereby the miniature rodent constructs its impregnable home:

On one trip I asked Dr. Loye Miller [of UCLA] how pack rats made nests of cholla stems. He prefaced his reply by stating that he was now Professor Emeritus. He said it was a very simple matter. Pack rats get in front of a segment of jumping cactus, teased it until it jumped and then the rat quickly moved to one side. By repeating the performance another cholla joint was added to the nest!

Many a desert hiker is probably prepared to believe the story of the jumping cactus after a few unpleasant encounters with it, but in actuality the industrious packrat is able to carry the joints using mouth and paws, after first nipping off the tips of the cactus needles wherever they are likely to puncture the rodent while in the act of transport. Careful inspection of the Cholla Garden reveals a network of packrat "runs" up and down and laterally along the cholla branches where many thousands of needle tips have been neatly blunted by the accuracy of the packrat's teeth.

Like the Bigelow cholla, the ocotillo (*Fouquieria splendens*) is endemic to the Sonoran Desert. The Ocotillo Patch, 1.5 miles east of the Cholla Garden, is one of the northernmost outposts of this unusual plant. Long, spindly, cane-like limbs covered with thorns, radiate from a central stub, giving the ocotillo the appearance of growing upside down with its roots waving madly in the air. A good rainstorm causes the normally bare limbs to burst forth with a close-fitting jacket of brilliant green leaves. In its most spectacular phase, usually in spring, the ocotillo sports crimson blossoms streaming like pennants from the tip of each of its limber flagpole branches.

Central Pinto Basin/Dale Road

East of the Ocotillo Patch the park highway descends into the very heart of Pinto Basin. To modern visitors traversing these miles of brush flats it seems incredible that man once attempted to transform this desolate valley into a setting of farms and communities. It happened in the 1920s when the Lake County Development Syndicate gained control of several sections of land in Pinto Basin and touted the region as the next great desert development. The company's seductive sales letter illustrates that real estate developers have not changed much with time:

> Dear Friend:
>
> We believe that PINTO BASIN is ready for an attempt at development. It adjoins Twenty-nine Palms Valley, where water is now a certainty, where land is rapidly being settled, where new farms and ranches are already in the making, where a small but excellent hotel is open the year 'round. New county highways are building, gasoline stations springing up to supply the increasing volume of traffic.
>
> A surprising number of Californians are learning the lure of the desert - learning its health-giving qualities - learning its myriad opportunities for recreation and crop productions and financial gain.
>
> Whether or not the desert attracts you as an individual, the fact remains, and cannot be disputed, that a veritable army of health-seekers, pioneer ranchers and INVESTORS are searching out every furthest valley in Southern California. The day of speculation and advancing prices of desert lands has arrived.
>
> We repeat - Pinto Basin is ripe today for an attempt at development. Even as raw desert land, it is well worth the price we ask. But our policy is to sell only such land as we conscientiously believe will show a profit to the purchaser - our client.
>
> So - acting on the best knowledge and advice it is possible to secure, we have arranged to drill for water, provided for funds for that purpose, and to place those funds in trust for your protection, so that in time to come we may see Pinto Basin changed from desert to highly developed ranches and farms.
>
> If desert land without water is a "buy" at these prices, then this should be an opportunity to be grasped by every investor who has the slightest knowledge of desert values and the increased prices which follow the discovery of WATER. Get YOURS while prices are at their present level - the lowest we will ever ask for this or similar land.
>
> Yours for success,
>
> LAKE COUNTY DEVELOPMENT SYNDICATE, Inc.

Fortunately Pinto Basin's meager water resources, combined with the Great Depression, failed to support the grandiose plans of its developers. Otherwise this peaceful valley with its timeless sense of solitude would have been lost forever.

Between the Ocotillo Patch and the Dale Road Junction lies Turkey Flat with its Backcountry Use Board (4.9 miles east of Ocotillo Patch, 12.0 miles west from Dale Road Junction). The picturesque name is derived from a short-lived attempt at poultry farming during those hopeful days of the 1920s. From Turkey Flat mountaineers set forth on the all-day climb of Pinto Mountain which dominates the skyline to the north. This should be attempted only by experienced hikers carrying plenty of extra water. Less ambitious hikers may choose to venture into the nearby sand dunes to the north. The visitor bound for either destination will find that kangaroo rats have constructed vast networks of tunnels just beneath the surface. Walking inevitably turns into a comical parody of the Saturday night inebriate as the hiker stumbles and plunges into these shallow excavations at every other step.

The Dale and Black Eagle roads turn off the park highway 7.1 miles north of the Cottonwood Spring Visitor Center. Neither road is maintained and local inquiry should be made before attempting to drive these routes. The ruins of Sunrise Well and the Sunrise Mill are located on the Dale Road 10.5 miles north of the junction. Beyond these ruins is the park boundary and the Dale mining district with its assortment of abandoned and active mines, and the inevitable "NO TRESPASSING" signs.

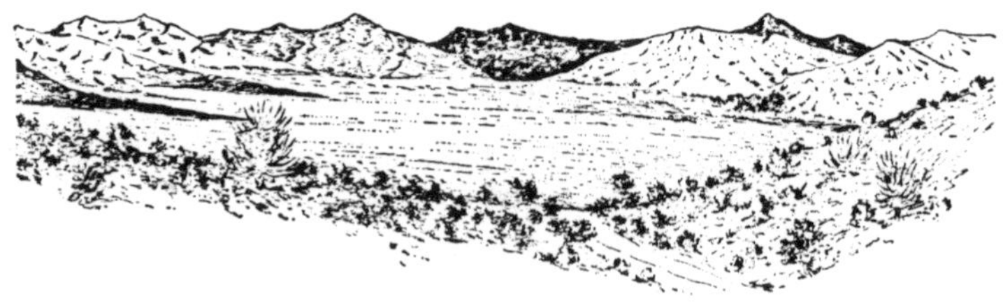

This is a beautiful little oasis, shut in by hills, and where half a dozen glorious old cottonwoods, dignified, hoary, and majestic, give gentle seclusion. Close by, seeping out of the rocks, is a steady though small supply of water, hence this has become one of the most noted resting places of the region.

George Wharton James
Wonders of the Colorado Desert, 1906

CHAPTER 20

AROUND COTTONWOOD SPRING

FEATURES: Matt Riley grave site, palm oasis, teamsters road, Morton's Mill site, Mastodon Mine, Winona Mill site, Lost Palms Oasis Trail.

Matt Riley's Last Trip

The temperature was 104 degrees Fahrenheit in Riverside on July 4, 1905, and undoubtedly hotter in Pinto Basin. The superintendent of the Dale District's Brooklyn Mine warned the two miners that it would be dangerous to cross the Basin on foot at this time of year, but

Matt Riley and Frank Kitto were determined men. They drew their wages and started out early that morning with the intention of following the teamsters road to Cottonwood Spring, "only" 26 miles away to the south. There they could hitch a ride on one of the freight wagons for which Cottonwood served as a regular depot. With any luck, they might be celebrating the Fourth in Indio that very evening.

It had sounded so simple only a few hours ago, as Matt Riley reflected on his present situation. The blazing sun beat down with a palpable weight. Kitto had become ill shortly after they had set out, falling by the wayside to rest before returning to the coolness of the Brooklyn mine shaft. Riley was stronger, and stubborn. As the sun approached its zenith, memories of his brother's horrible death by heat and thirst on the Amboy Road several years prior may have intruded on Riley's rambling thoughts. Why hadn't he reached Cottonwood Spring yet? There was Eagle Mountain, right where the superintendent had said it would be. But which of the wagon tracks leads to the spring?

In a real life game where close doesn't count, Riley did better than many whose graves lie scattered over the desert. In his final delirious wanderings he came within 200 yards of the life-saving water source, only to have the invisible hand of the desert pull him back into its bosom. A teamster discovered his shrunken remains and buried Riley where he fell, next to a juniper bush that casts some comforting shade on the unfortunate miner's last resting place. Desert hikers can visit

Matt Riley's Grave

Riley's grave, and ponder their own preparedness. It is located a quarter-mile north of the Cottonwood Visitor Center, about 20 yards east of the park highway. The lonely site lies beside the faint trace of the old teamsters road to Cottonwood Spring.

Cottonwood Spring

In Matt Riley's day over 3000 gallons of water a day flowed from Cottonwood Spring. Today the spring barely seeps. Earthquakes and subtle land shifts have greatly affected the spring over the decades, but apparently there has always been some water at or near the surface. The big palms and cottonwood trees attest to this, as do the presence of Indian artifacts such as bedrock mortars. Two exceptional examples of these Indian grinding holes may be inspected just a few paces from the spring, located in boulders sitting about 15 feet to the right of the Lost Palms Oasis Trail where it starts up the hill from Cottonwood Spring, no more than 100 feet from the cluster of trees around the oasis. Only the rocks themselves could tell how many generations it took to wear the mortars so deeply into the hard stone.

To the people who came to work and live in the mining districts of Dale, the Eagle Mountains and the Hexies - and especially to the teamsters who hauled all the necessities required to maintain these remote outposts - Cottonwood Spring was an important center of activity. Here was located one of only two reliable water sources between the mines and Mecca, the nearest railroad depot. Prior to the development of Shaver's Well a few miles to the south, Cottonwood was the one and only water supply.

The mine owners often went to incredible extremes to obtain water, stringing pipelines across miles of barren desert to obtain a supply of the precious liquid. J. Smeaton Chase traveled through Cottonwood in the early decades of the twentieth century and recorded a colorful description of the oasis and one of its inhabitants:

> As I was saddling up for an early start, a Crusoe-like figure appeared on the hill above a doorless cabin that I had decided to be uninhabited. The old man proved to be a caretaker in charge of the machinery which pumps water from this place to a mine eighteen miles to the east. (Such are the difficulties that must be overcome before these desert mines can be worked.) . . . Cottonwood Springs is one of the few desert watering-places at which the traveller would wish to stay longer than necessity requires. Some bygone hermit had planted a few apple trees, which promised a tolerable crop, and there was even a garden patch where Crusoe cultivated radishes, beans, and tomatoes for the benefit of the local quail and jack-rabbits. An old arrastra (the primitive means of crushing ore in a circular pit, by dragging heavy weights over it, with horse or mule for motive power) spoke of old times and timers, and the samples of rock scattered about would have furnished several museums with specimens. My friend's conversation bore all upon mining affairs and was Hebrew to me; while mine no doubt was equally worthless to him, for the desert had dried out every interest but one, and turned him into a sort of mineral. [*California Desert Trails*, 1919]

Perhaps it was Chase's Crusoe, or a teamster passing through, who planted the palm trees. No early visitor to Cottonwood Spring ever mentioned the presence of these striking plants. An unattributed source in the park archives indicates the palms were planted around 1920.

Teamsters Road and Morton's Mill Site

An easy foot-journey originating at Cottonwood Spring will give the visitor a flavor of what it might have been like to pilot a freight wagon into the desert wilderness. Begin by heading down the wash leading from Cottonwood Spring. The flat area immediately downstream from the spring formerly contained Cottonwood Campground. Severe impact on the plant life surrounding the spring posed a problem that could only be solved by removing the camp to the high ground it now occupies. Below the flat, Cottonwood Canyon narrows and turns to the left, entering an enchanting passage between high rock walls decorated with cholla and ocotillos. Soon the old teamsters road is encountered where it exits the wash to the right, just before the dry waterfall that prevented wagon travel directly through the canyon. The bypass around the waterfall remains in a good state of preservation. When one walks down the farther side of the bypass it becomes obvious what backbreaking labor went into its construction. George Wharton James came this way and had few kind words to say of the bypass:

> . . . owing to the rains it [Cottonwood Canyon] was full of rich beauty when we went through it twice in April, 1906. There were the ironwood, the palo verde, and a few mesquite, with the ever-present creosote bush in full flower.
>
> When near to Cottonwood Springs - not more than half a mile away if one were able to go directly over the range - the road used to make a wide detour around, of some three or four miles. The county officials were requested to construct a road over the short route, but with a stupidity that seems incredible, instead of having the county engineer or surveyor direct the work and expend enough money to make an easy graded well-built road, they put the job into the hands of a local politician who spent three or four hundred dollars of the county's money in constructing what the teamsters call a "Chilcoot Pass," and over which only extra well-equipped wagons can pass. A light buggy with a good horse can go over with little trouble, but a two-horse wagon with an ordinary load finds it practically impossible. [*Wonders of the Colorado Desert*, 1906]

To stand atop this old grade and imagine driving a laden wagon with mules or horses straining at their traces is to understand why it came to be called Little Chilcoot Pass, after the infamously steep Yukon portal used by the Klondike gold-seekers of 1898.

The sandy wash below Little Chilcoot Pass is home to a wide variety of handsome plants. Mesquites, palo verdes, and smoke trees dominate; in spring, chuparosa bushes burst out in crimson arrays, and the floor of the wash becomes carpeted with chia, canterbury bells, blazing stars and other short-lived annuals.

A quarter-mile beyond the lower end of the Little Chilcoot grade are the ruins of Morton's Mill site, located on an embankment on the right (west) side of the wash. The rusting tanks remain from the 1930s when "Cactus" "Slim" Morton operated a modest stamp mill servicing nearby mines that were temporarily active during the Depression.

Cottonwood Wash looking upstream at the Teamsters Road

Mastodon Peak Trail

You can't see forever, but the view from Mastodon Peak (named by miners for its fancied resemblance to the prehistoric beast) does take in an impressive piece of desert. A 3-mile loop trail takes hikers nearly to the top of the peak and returns them via the ruins of the Mastodon Mine and the Winona Mill site.

The route begins at Cottonwood Spring, following the Lost Palms Oasis Trail for 0.6 mile to its junction with the Mastodon Peak Trail. Turning left onto the latter, another half mile brings one to a viewpoint just below the last stony battlements of Mastodon Peak. The summit scramble is most easily accomplished around the right-hand side of the outcrop.

From the viewpoint, the trail descends a short distance to the inclined shaft and massive timbers marking the site of the Mastodon Mine. Sporadically active between 1919 and 1932, some of the Mastodon gold ore assayed as high as $744 per ton. The mine seemed destined for a rosy future until the ore body was severed by a fault close to the surface.

A mile beyond the Mastodon Mine is the site of Winona, a village that flourished briefly during the 1920s. Some of Winona's inhabitants worked at the Mastodon Mine, but most of them labored at the ball mill that processed ore from a number of mines in the vicinity. The trail passes beside the concrete foundations of the mill before descending into the tree-shaded dell that sheltered the community. Cottonwoods and exotic plants, such as eucalyptus and pomegranates, planted by the millhands and their families, have grown to provide a cool respite for today's hikers.

A quarter-mile past Winona is the junction with the Cottonwood Campground Nature Trail. The left fork returns to the Cottonwood Spring parking lot; the right branch leads to the campground.

Lost Palms Oasis

Lost Palms Canyon contains one of the two largest assemblages of native fan palms (*Washingtonia filifera*) in the park. (The other large group occurs in Munsen Canyon, a wild gorge accessible from Lost Palms Canyon via a rugged cross-country hike.) The Lost Palms Oasis Trail is shadeless and no water is available either enroute or at the oasis, so it is necessary to carry plenty of fluid refreshment (up to a gallon a day per person in hot weather). This 8-mile round-trip hike should be reserved for winter and early spring days when the morning chill serves to stimulate muscular activity. Under these conditions there are few other desert treks that can offer as much beauty.

The Lost Palms Trail begins at Cottonwood Spring, climbs into a region of rolling hills alternating with sandy washes, and finally plunges several hundred feet into the lovely palm grove nestled between the walls of Lost Palms Canyon. (Note: The uphill climb back out of the canyon is the most strenuous part of the hike.) Eroded buttes and towers, balanced rocks, and a rich display of desert flora provide much interest along the way. Plants representative of both the Mojave and Colorado deserts grow side by side - Mojave yucca, ocotillos, junipers, desert willows, native palms and various chollas; and ephemeral annuals such as Mojave aster, desert mallow, lupines, scarlet locoweed, and that miniature perfection, the golden coreopsis.

By beginning early in the day there is time to amble along the trail and enjoy a relaxing lunch beneath the palms. With luck, the most beautiful music of the desert may be heard, the eery rustle of palm fronds stirred by a canyon breeze.

INDEX